AF227984

LOOK AN ELEPHANT IN THE EYE

By

Louise Usher

After Asia
Part of the "After Travel" series

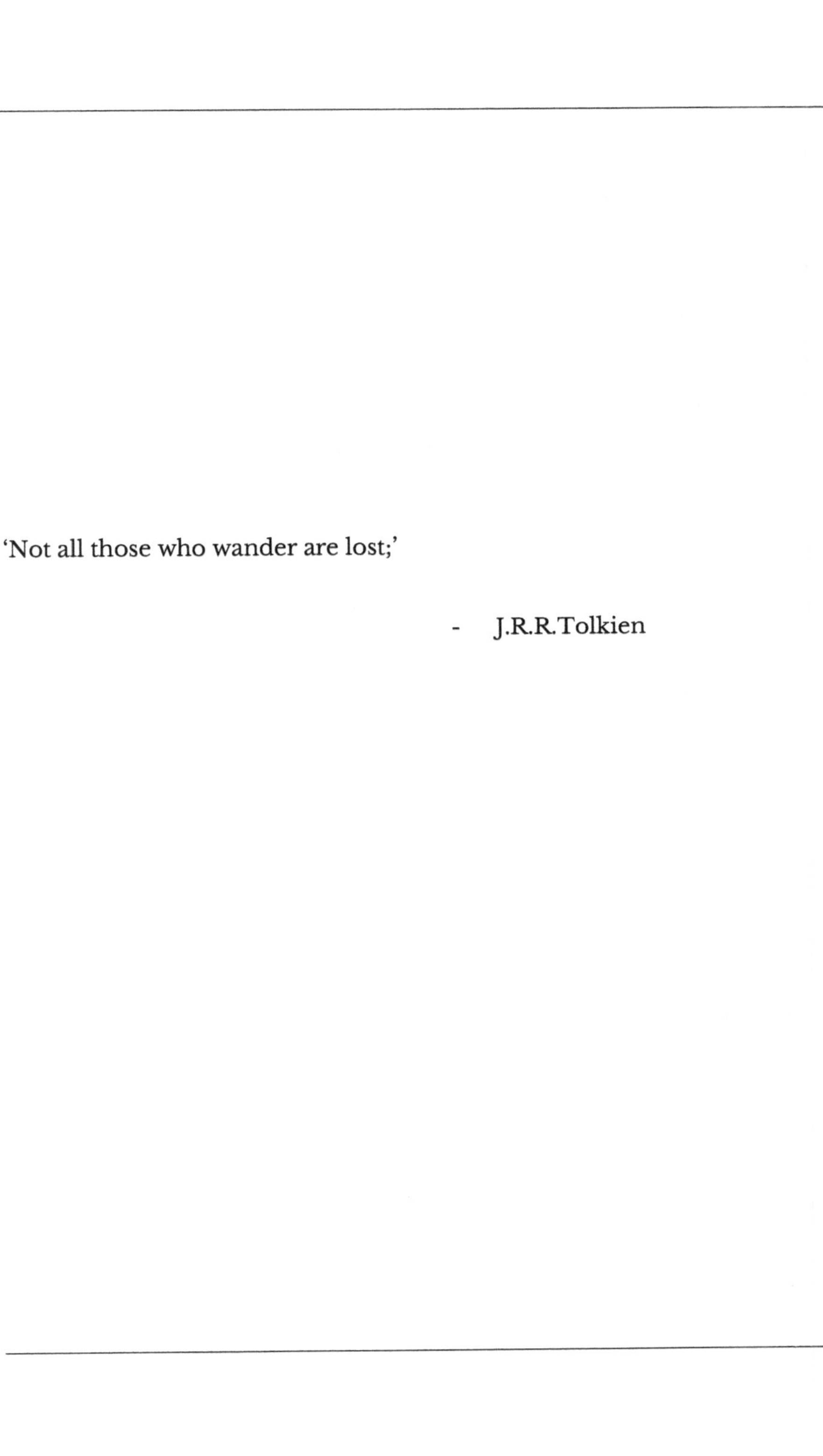

'Not all those who wander are lost;'

-    J.R.R.Tolkien

Contents

ACKNOWLEDGEMENTS

About the author

Also by this author

This book is dedicated to those I've had the pleasure to share a coffee (or a coconut) with

Prologue

T"They will never forget, but you have to look them straight in the eye," my ex-husband told me. He was taking care of things while we were away.

'Things' mostly related to Mum and the care she needed. My son and my ex-husband would share tasks, and I was glad to have them. I gave thanks enough for both Mum and I that they would be stepping in.

After eight years of caring for Mum, I had believed I was exhausted. After returning from the trip to Southeast Asia, I'd come to know a different level of exhaustion; a weariness beyond what words could capture. Perhaps it had been frustration, perhaps resignation, or just the constant edge of worry. Looking back, I was a simmering kettle of fatigue. It had been a gruelling year, and I was searching for ways to keep myself afloat, keep happy enough to survive and keep positive there was a future ahead for me. I was tired of fighting.

"I looked back up at the elephant when we were in India and I wondered what might happen if he stood on me. They are bloody huge, you know. Then he," he interrupted himself for a cough, a signal of impending exaggeration, "reared up on his back legs and I thought shit, he's going to stand on me." Despite the half-truth, the elephants size haunted my thoughts. Could I be courageous enough to let myself be awed, to face the enormity of life and fully explore it, not just survive it? This trip was not just about exploration; it was about proving something to myself. I'd been inspired by stories where journeys turn inward just as much as they turn outward, and I hoped Asia might hold the same clarity for me. I reminded myself to go lightly on expectations.

"Nah, it will be nice," I said, remembering the brief I had given to my daughter Jasmine. I had typed into the search box on my laptop, 'Eat Pray Love elephant scene.' The little piece of film I found was cut and ended too quickly. It showed Julia Roberts' characters fear, and the delight which followed as she scrambled to her feet. While sitting in silence, she watched a painted elephant walking towards her, and she must have wondered what was going to happen next. The memoir was one of my favourites to read, and the film adaptation was a delight to watch.

A journey of discovery had unfolded in front of us as we watched Liz purposefully figure out life. I related to many of the tales within the story, and I wondered if my trip to Asia would result in a new book. This trip was about living, not capturing. I decided not to place too much importance on a new story, after working on a previous story, Whitewashed, for over a year.

The world was waiting for me to explore it, while I could, before long plane rides became too uncomfortable.

I arranged a part of the tour about a year ago. A part of me didn't believe I would be going. I had apologised to my students that I wouldn't be there for their final poster presentations.

"I'll be in Thailand," I told them as I grinned. It felt like a lie. But I couldn't deny myself the plans once our bags were being loaded in the car. We were driven to Heathrow airport for the first leg of an eight-part journey. Even though I travelled to hotels abroad for part of my work, this felt brand new. I had never 'gone travelling' before. This was a long trip, and I had packed carefully to navigate those essential items, including the things I needed if I had a flare up.

Jasmine and I took more selfies than we needed outside of the departures gate. We had initially thought we would be the only ones in our group to fly out so early, but there were dozens of messages every day in the group chat showing videos of tiger sharks from way below the surface of the water. I flipped up the vlog camera and repeated, "I'm not sure I have ever been this excited for a trip."

Deciding to call it a holiday gave me permission to be public about it. When I travelled for work, random people would message wishing me a delightful holiday. To avoid defending myself, I had stopped telling people I was away. Many onlookers seemed to expect me to sit at Mum's side, head cocked to one side, rubbing her arm in sympathy. I felt judged.

When I was away with work, there was always time to walk in the shoreline, or sit with a longer lunch than usual, but it was never a holiday. My mind would race with ideas for how to review the hotel. I would be up before dawn to carry out the filming I needed, so I didn't disturb the people who were on holiday, and I would do my best to ensure I was as true and fair as possible. I loved that job, but if I was honest with myself, it wasn't quite covering the mortgages on mine and Mum's house. I wanted to continue to support my family, but I needed more money to deal with the hikes in interest rates.

I was tired of thinking of new ideas. So, it was time to forget all of that for a few weeks and instead, marvel at the world.

Heathrow Terminal Four was fancy. Designer shops lined the walkway, including a Mont Blanc shop, with various pens. I had only recently paid my last Mont Blanc off, which was a treat to myself for passing my MA. I looked, didn't touch, and left the shop again.

I had opted not to use special assistance for this trip, as it only seemed reasonable if you needed a wheelchair. I was resisting that idea, despite the advice from the occupational therapist. The unwanted delivery of the wheelchair they brought six years previously was now being used by Mum.

"You should really only walk about ten minutes with AS before getting into the wheelchair," they told me. I could hear echoes of 'use it or lose it' going around in my head. With plenty of stretching, nutrition and other lifestyle tweaks, I was sure I could keep out of that chair.

Fancy cars resembling 'Brum' from the 1990s disguised as golf carts took people around the airport. We took photos and videos of everything. We beamed with wide smiles and called out to each other to look here and see there. I wished my son could have joined us.

Tracking our suitcases using air tags, I could see they were travelling faster than us through the airport and onto the plane. Despite having months to prepare for this trip, I did wonder if I had organized the packing as well as I should have.

"Let's have a look." Jasmine pointed to the announcement board with the long list of departures on it.

"Twenty-two," I said. "Twenty-minute walk?" I sneered and knew it would not take twenty minutes. We began our journey towards Abu Dhabi with a few more photos on the travelator before we saw a big brown jet ahead of us.

"That's our plane, is that our plane?" Jasmine said.

It was. It was massive. I got the idea of how large it was out of my anxious mind. I wasn't anxious really. I was experiencing intrusive thoughts. I knew this from my training as a coach. I had to dig deep to be brave.

To see the world would take courage.

Flying

Several months before, one autumn evening, Jasmine and I flipped up the laptop at the dining room table.

Looking at flights on the laptop, we could see that one of the major airlines was the cheapest flight we could find. To double check this was not a mistake, we had a brief look on YouTube, to see videos of people who had flown with them. The plane looked luxurious, and the food was exquisite. One vlog we saw even detailed a suite on the plane, the Airbus A380. How far we have come in the world of aviation, to have a sofa, bed, and even a top notch turn down service on a plane. We wouldn't be booking the suite this time, or business class, but I was hopeful I may be lucky enough to get an upgrade on one of the four flights we were about to book. Only one plane would be the Airbus. We booked it as the last flight, back from the Asia tour, and I figured it was something to be excited about on the way home, and buffer our disappointment.

We looked up a map of the airbus on the website. It had five prayer rooms. If they were multi-faith, I would go there to pray. What a unique experience that would be.

Occasionally, some planes flew directly to Bangkok, but these were slightly more expensive, and we were careful to budget, in order to cram in as much as we possibly could. We booked the plane, looked at each other and grinned.

"We are going to Thailand, Jas," I said.

"Thailand Mum."

It seemed as if it would be so far into the future, that it was impossible to fathom that it would actually happen. Before we even considered packing, there was a lot of planning to do. Ideally, we would be gone for four weeks. We would visit several countries. I justified spending the money with a reminder I had to cash in my private pension early. Thankfully, my GP could approve the forms to say my health was getting in the way of working like a trojan horse. Even though we were looking at less than £10,000 pay out, it was something which would help me pay mortgages on both houses while Mum was still alive. It was a worrying time. Mortgage rates had sorn in the previous two years. I wasn't the only one finding things hard. I was glad of the pension payout. To spend it all on mortgage repayments felt as though life was cheating me slightly. This was my only private pension. To take £1500 from the pot to pay for the Asia trip took the sting out of the situation.

The trip felt like a pipe dream, but we got excited right away.

1

Wonka

I stood in Heathrow airport, at the side of the travelator at gate 22, looking at the huge brown jet. It was time.

Our organized carry-on bags allowed us to put the remaining items above us in the overhead locker. We had enough leg room to keep moving during the next six or seven hours, and we decided we would watch Wonka together. The film was different to the other Wonka films. A plethora of visual opposites took us on a journey in Wonka's mind, from the struggle of reality, which was muddy and brown, to the imagination of the dream he carried with a palette of colours in a fantasy shop full of magical sweets and chocolates. Reality or imagination was something I struggled with for many years, and I related to Wonka and his determination to continue to believe, even when reality was so far removed from what he could see inside his mind. Life bobbed to the surface on many occasions when I was living the torture of being a creative. I would do the sensible things and aim to keep juggling all the necessary rules which were put in place to try to navigate this tricky life. Inside, my soul was dying. My spirit wanted me to embrace the creative who tapped from inside my mind every so often. I went through a meander of turns from health that forced me to be less physical, to opened doors of people asking me to fulfil a need they had, which embraced my creative imagination.

My inner child played more these days. A few years before, she was released as I unknowingly entered a period of inner work when I fell in love. I was never sure if his purpose in my life was to open up the little girl inside who was still walking with heavy shoulders. Was I reading a story which wasn't there? Is life as simple as doing what feels good? For some people, that might be gardening, for others, it's clocking in and out of work at certain times of the day. For me, it's picking up a pen and writing. Add in a coffee shop, with the white noise behind me and I am in a colourful bubble of joy. This happy place was somewhere I wanted to be every day, and I had dreamed of this since I was old enough to write.

Just like Wonka, the occasional doubt crept in.

What if people hated my work?

What if it failed?

What if people were nasty about things I had written?

They were nasty to everyone. There was always nastiness, and I didn't know how to avoid it. How did EL avoid it? I was about to meet her at a publishing conference. Excited to soak up some of the energy coming from her, I wanted to see the woman who brought one of the greatest love stories I had seen in my lifetime. Not every reader or film critic 'got it'. I did. I understood the love story more than I could ever publicly admit.

Fear had kept me from publishing more. Covid times saw the last best seller, and it felt as though I was living my best life. Editing and writing all day, walking for miles, not having to interact with others, lighting candles and sitting with Harley and a coffee while I wrote were my ideal days. I was clear about my ideal life. I knew what it looked like, and I couldn't deny the joy I felt on the days I was writing. I felt like it was my calling. It wasn't about making millions, or even being overly popular and selling thousands of books, but it was about changing lives. Perhaps it had finally come later in life so I could experience some darn awful stuff to write about. They call that 'having some gas in the tank' in the writer world.

Friends were few in my life. But some of them were golden. One in particular became a friend after she became a colleague. And she was an academic, like me, but she did not stop beating the drum about me and my calling. Polar opposite to teaching science, but the creative in me couldn't help but agree with her.

"I mean, the PhD isn't giving you anything except stress and it if isn't your purpose, why would you want to pursue it?" I agreed with her and said I was going to be focusing on writing more stories in the hope it would fuel others to live a better life. We discussed TV shows on the popular channel called Gaia. All day long, we could talk about energy, things we didn't know about, and that spiritual feeling one carries inside. She told me about one show I must definitely watch, and I had put it on my list.

One evening, I was on the sofa, not long after we lost my beloved Harley, and I tried to sign up to Gaia. My membership had lapsed, and I was keen to watch this programme. She text the title of it to me. I used the remote control to sign up, and I entered the details on my credit card three times. Three times, it didn't work. The credit card was blocked, and it took weeks to be able to use it again. I was flowing, nothing would stop me from watching this programme, and I decided to search on YouTube for the same programme. I found it. My hand automatically reached out to celebrate with Harley. He wasn't there. I sighed and clicked play on YouTube. But this was a different show.

Dr Lipton, who I was a fan of, was presenting. The message inside the video was surely divine. One sentence spoke to me as he said that people who watch Gaia are the ones who can help to heal the planet. My expertise wasn't climate change, or the war, or the state of the planet, but I did feel a chaotic disconnect. I had questioned my 'calling' as a writer in the past. I knew it was something I was destined to do, but I had never quite understood why in totality. It felt very basic to say I was going to write to help people and change lives. It was true, but I felt there was something bigger, something more.

My thoughts wandered to a place of knowing about vibrational energy, and automatic writing. I could write and inspire a select few people, just a few, and raise their vibration from one of despair, and that energy would reflect on the energy of the planet. Would it? I didn't question it at the time, as it felt so clear and so definite that I had found the reason for my purpose. I knew my calling was to write, although I wasn't sure why. Now I felt I knew why. Raising the vibration of a select few would help to raise the vibration of the mother earth.

Wonka didn't have a smooth journey. There were obstacles to navigate, but he was determined. I needed to dig deep inside and find my own encouragement. I questioned if I had the energy.

2

Abu Dhabi Airport

When we arrived at Abu Dhabi airport, I was astounded by sights which fuelled my gasps. People were in a smoking booth, like an enclosed place you see on the side of the train station in outer London, to protect you from the rain. As we looked closer, it seemed clear in there. There was no smoke lingering in the air. We didn't want to seem rude and stare, but this phenomenon was incredible. Singapore was supposed to be ahead of the times, but so was Abu Dhabi. People could squeeze in and enjoy a cigarette without polluting the air or having to leave and go outside. The smoke was extracted somehow.

If travellers were on a stopover, like us, and they were smokers, they would need something 'airside', or go without. All our luggage was dealt with and we didn't need to go through passport control or security. After our three-hour stop over, we headed back to the plane and considered if it was the same plane or not. We suspected it was, which would make sense.

To the left of the travelator was a holder with four compartments. Each contained a black pushchair, for those people with little children.

"Here, this is for you little Jas," I laughed as I pointed the camera towards the buggies. Jas laughed and we both looked at each other with a sparkle in our eyes. We had flown all night and barely slept, but you could see that our spirits felt like four-year-olds at Christmas. We were determined to keep the long journey as part of the adventure rather than something to be endured to reach the pot of gold at the end of the rainbow.

My camera was digesting all the shops, including a chocolate café which failed at calling me in, and I thought about my YouTube audience as two men passed the lens. Head to toe in white, with little black discs on top of their heads. I didn't dictate to the camera as I wasn't sure what you would respectfully call these men. Were they sheikhs? Or just local citizens, dressed appropriately for the weather? I wasn't sure. There was a lot to learn before we returned for our stop over on the way home in a few week's time. It seemed forever away, and I wasn't sure which part of the trip I was more excited about.

Neither of us felt like eating anything as Etihad served us twice on the last flight, and we suspected they would serve us twice again on the next leg. We felt good. We had energy, fitness and our vibration was high. Passing the first-class Etihad lounge, we sat in the seats close by, which reminded me of the heated loungers at the gym I used to go to. They laid back, and I realised that was a genius piece of engineering for those of us who sometimes swelled up a little on the plane. Legs almost above the heart, I did my best to take care of my body before we boarded the next plane.

21

3

Bangkok

In the distance, the lights strung like coloured pearls as we came in to land on the Thailand tarmac for the first time. Feeling good, we gathered our bags as one of the last people to leave the plane. My mind realised I didn't know what was next.

We had sat for hours and hours, having many meetings, organising flights, hotels, different websites and competition partners. Watching YouTube had given us ideas of what we wanted to do, and what we were less bothered about.

My usual routine with travel, the other day job, was to travel as part of a package deal, and that was easy. You would find a rep and figure out your bus number before sitting and waiting at the transfer, soaking up the new weather.

Bangkok was beckoning us, with ease. The passport checkers, police, smiled at us and said thank you. Unique. I cocked my head to the side as I looked at Jasmine on the other side of security. I approvingly turned down my mouth and raised my eyebrows to show her my surprise at the manner of the first Thai people we had just encountered.

"Ok then." I flipped my head backwards in silence to suggest my joy. "Right, what now? Where do we go?"

We had both bought ESims, on the suggestion of many online platforms. A deal I had simmering had fallen through by one ESim company. They planned to sponsor two videos, for not very much money. Offering two free ESims for Jas and me, for the totality of the trip, I agreed, but I felt a little reluctant. People didn't seem to like advertising on any platforms these days unless it was an official TV show, and I had been subject to some hate on my last series on YouTube when I went to Tunisia for three nights to review an all-inclusive hotel. One of the people who used a couple is of my Facebook groups to research the hotels he wanted to go to had started to publicly ask questions about how much I earned for my affiliate marketing. I would happily share that the most I had ever earned was £200 for a month, including all of my YouTube ad revenue and affiliate links. But the Facebook groups and YouTube editing took at least 30 hours of my time each week and had done for around six years. So, pretty much, it was a voluntary role. I felt this was a rude question, and not many people would consider asking. The guy started to venture onto every platform and put messages on there for all to see, highlighting the 1-4% payment for each sale, listing my different online platforms, and pretty much bullying me for trying to do a job. Thousands, millions, of people work online now. This man was closer to seventy years old judging by his profile photos and maybe he just didn't understand. Inside, I wanted to protest and let him know that my working world is limited due to my health, and yet I have no help to pay for Mum, her care and her living expenses and I'm trying to keep my family afloat. But this would just seem defensive, which it was. Who really cares that much to be so nasty? I'm not asking him to pay me. I'm putting out free information, at my own expense and actions like this just contributed to keeping my vibe low, depressed and want to cry. There were many days when I wanted to throw in the towel. Life felt too hard. I tried to juggle things and try new things. But people like that seem more prevalent in the world and every online creator is likely subject to hate and nasty comments. I wish I could just brush them off. Was it me, or them? Whose issue was this?

The guy I had struck the deal with was sacked from the ESim company and I felt uneasy. I did reach out to reply to the next salesperson, but by which time I had started to listen to that inner voice which was telling me I really didn't like sponsorships. I was agreeing to them for the sake of earning some money, to pay for two mortgages. And if I could stop doing it, I would. I wondered what would happen if I focused elsewhere and told the ESim company I wouldn't be creating sponsored videos for them. Instead, we signed up with a new company, paid for our ESims easily. It was cheap and technically straight forward.

After airport security, we pulled out our phones and checked. We had internet. We had the Grab app downloaded which meant we could get around if needed, and we had £400 worth of Thai Baht in our bags, half each.

The airport was very busy and a little dusty in places. We hadn't appreciated the air conditioning until we left through the revolving doors later on. There was a line of people waving clipboards, pointing at hand-made posters which were draped over the barriers, and people waving their hands and calling out, "taxi, taxi."

Forgetting the name of the hotel we were booked to stay in, I nodded my head to let Jas know we needed to find a quieter corner, and I pulled my suitcase along behind me.

"Ok, let's take a minute," I said. We both nodded and breathed. "What do we need to do next?" I asked out loud, while taking the straps of my backpack off my shoulders. I had a blue plastic folder with every hotel, plane and trip booking printed out. At the top of each of the pieces of paper I had written the date. I popped open the clasp and looked for the ones after the Etihad flight info, dated May 17th.

I leaned against the wall which was coated in a wipeable plastic material and I took enough of a breath that it felt like a moment. Breathing out, I grinned to my daughter who looked as fresh as when she had just left home. Her eyes twinkled. No words passed between us. Glancing back down to my organised papers, I saw the second piece of carefully folded paper had the hotel name written on it.

"Hotel Suvarnabhumi Ville Airport," I said as I laughed the airport name incorrectly. I was sure I didn't name it properly. My mind wandered to a conversation at a dance event a few weeks before,

"Yeah, cos if I fly straight to BKK airport, then I can just get a cab or a bus to the hotel, cos BKK airport is closer than the other one. Yeh. I think I will book to fly to BKK airport, straight there."

I looked our dance friend in the eyes and smiled, "now say the actual airport name, James." We all laughed. Two airports in Bangkok alone, we knew this was going to be a big city.

Any hotel costing £28.27 was always going to raise inquiry into its quality, but now we had a name, and I could search up how close it was by using our carefully crafted ESim, and my spectacle-less eyes which could just about keep up with the map.

"I reckon we could walk there Jas," I said. I started to reach behind me to pull my suitcase back into the chaos of the hotel reps calling out. Assuming they would all speak English; I waved the printed paper in the direction of one lady and asked about the hotel name.

"Ah yes, you will need to. Um. Wait," she pointed, "over there, up there," she prodded her hand in the air as if we had to go a long way.

"Can we walk there?"

"Wait. Come." She instructed us to follow her, and she didn't walk as fast as I suspected she usually did. We walked past a revolving doorway which gave a blast of heat, but there was no time to glance at Jasmine and comment on the heat. We needed to concentrate. After several steps, the chaos elevated to a different level and we heard shouting in accents, hotel names, people selling taxis and sim cards.

"You need sim?" We were asked. I barely glanced up. I looked as shy as Princess Diana and carried on walking.

"Here," our host pointed. We looked at the end of her finger and trailed a look towards the crash barriers where hotel names were draped. "No. Come." She realised that wasn't the right place. "Here, here." She spoke in Thai to a man who was stood in front of us. They didn't communicate with us that this was the rep for the hotel Ville we were staying at. We were beckoned outside.

Jas and I were focused, but wanted time to reflect on this city, and our first taste of Thailand. But I was as nervous as a first day at college. You know it will be ok really, but you just don't know what to expect. Sirens echoed through the underground area we were jogging through, and red and blue lights flashed in the distance. The man waved to someone in a minibus and a small white bus pulled in close to us, with the hotel name etched on the side.

As soon as our bags were in the back, the man sat down and took a breath, as if he was as glad as us to be out of the savages of crazy Bangkok. This was exactly how I imagined it. Within seconds, Jasmine and I had tightened our seatbelts, and leaned back and held hands. I grinned, we sighed. Air conditioning was welcome. The bus was very cold. A young girl shared the journey with us. She had no suitcase, just a huge backpack. I gathered we would see a lot of backpackers.

The roads had at least four lanes on each side and we raced through the streets in a fast but organised stream. Within half a minute I saw a bridge ahead of us; it glimmered. As we got closer, we could see the bridge was covered in gold and had many figurines on it. I smiled and continued to look out of the window.

"I guess we are going to see lots of this type of thing."

Within less than ten minutes, we could tell we had pulled into a street which was lined with hotels. The driver clicked the indicator on, and we saw red and green fairy lights ahead of us, draped over some bushes. A silence fell in the bus. I stared at the lights and the edges of my mouth turned upwards as my teeth showed through a wide smile. This looked ok, for a £27 hotel stay.

It hadn't occurred to me to settle in too much, as we were on the way back in less than eight hours. I certainly wasn't expecting too much. But after gathering our cases from the driver, we heaved our bags up a steep ramp, leaning forwards at an exaggerated angle, and into a very cold reception, where a relaxed smile was waiting for us. The welcome was casual, and Jas and I asked him to repeat what he said,

"this voucher for free fruit platter. Top floor and fire show. Go to lift and up there," he pointed. He described this nonchalantly. We responded with 'ok,' as we settled the hotel bill. I had booked online with a 'pay at property' quote. Our local cash currency was part of the budget included to pay for both this hotel, and the other Bangkok hotel which was towards the end of our trip. At the reception desk, the concierge told us the transfer was 100 Thai Baht, and we were not at all sure if this was a rip off or not. We looked at each other, searching for answers, but accepted this price anyway. Later, we double checked, and the price was £2.14 which wouldn't even be the starting meter price in London. Getting used to such bargain prices would be easy, and a welcome relief after things being so difficult at home the past two years.

Jasmine and I had discussed dropping our bags to the room before heading up to the top floor, as the fire show was in ten minutes time.

During our research, we found fire shows were prevalent in Koh Samui, and we were excited to see those, but we would still take a lovely welcome such as this one. Especially with free fruit to accompany the view. Friends of ours had been sharing updates from Phi Phi, and we had seen the fruit was in abundance, and that included dragon fruit. The pink beauty had become a slight symbol of this trip for us, so we got in the lift as fast as we could drag our bags. It was hot in there. My eyes widened as I felt the lift move from one side to the other. 'Please don't break down', I thought. How long could you survive in that heat, I wondered.

Our bedroom was incredible. It was large, and clean enough. Jasmine checked the corners of the sheets to see if any little black dots resided there. This was her usual routine. Nothing. Just one little cockroach in the bathroom, which was faster than me, but not faster than the shower head. I hoped he wasn't harmed as I blasted him down the holes.

"oooooeew," Jasmine said. This was, so far, what we had expected in parts, and surpassed our expectations in other places. This hotel bed passed the knuckle press test and felt as though it would be comfy. The middle of the mattress had a body pillow which looked as if it was for us to keep our bodies separated, which we weren't fussed about. At home, I loved a body pillow as it was a game changer for my AS.

"This is all going so well, so smoothly."

"Yeah, it is Mum," Jas looked whiter now, but still illuminated.

"Let's film quickly, like, super quick. Then run up," I said as if it was a question. A large part of this trip was to grow that online following. I was determined. Not only would it give me a brilliant lifestyle, but it was a service which no one else was particularly doing, and certainly not those with my qualifications. Views meant income which meant more content and more income.

"Hello everyone, I am so excited to tell you I am filming this in Bangkok, in Thailand!" I started to talk to the camera before the room tour of the Suvarnabhumi Ville Hotel, before we locked up and headed back into the hot lift.

"He said it is the fourth floor, which is the roof." I hadn't realised that. I also was unaware of the views which laid waiting for us. The lift doors opened out to a room which was dark and black with mirrors. Walking through the indoors we followed a path which took us to the musty air outside. Warm white fairy lights cascaded across an obelisk of plastic bush plants, and I announced that we needed photographs. A staff member looked on without trying to hide his stares, then he bowed. His thumbs hooked underneath his chin as he created a praying shape with his hands. I hadn't realised this was something they actually did, for real. But they did. We were unaware of how delighted they would be to see us return the gesture and we said a simple hello. Climbing some more stairs, an impressive city scape was in front of us. Jasmine had our fruit voucher in her hands, and we were more excited than we should have been to exchange that with them. I wasn't sure if mumbled words were spoken or if there was a lot of waving around between us and the staff, but I fathomed English was not as readily spoken as it was in other countries we had visited. Nonetheless, we ended up with a front row seat, in front of some other couples. A little battery-operated crystal lamp was delivered to the table. This was it. We were living it. It was happening now, and the dream was more incredible than I had imagined.

There was dragon fruit, the sweetest pineapple I had ever tasted, a delightful mocktail and a ten-minute taster fire show.

There was an iconic trip to the 7 eleven close by, and a quick look at some street food.

There was the comfiest bed I had slept in and a pretty good shower, which wasn't shared with any cockroaches.

Then, there was a plane to Koh Samui on a tarmac close by.

4

Next stop, Samui

Eyes half closed; we sat on the sofa in reception. The cold created goose bumps and we were glad our hoodies were in our hand luggage. Next to us, the Irish lady with the large backpack sat down without making a sound. My gaze stayed on my handbag until I heard her, and Jasmine begin to chat. They must have made eye contact and possibly smiled at each other before they began to talk.

"Off back to the airport?"

"Yes, we are flying to Koh Samui today."

"Ah nice. I'm going to Koh Pangnan."

I frowned silently. You could only get to Koh Pangnan by boat, via Koh Samui. In theory, she wasn't wrong, but I was concerned that she was either lost or unsure that she was going via Koh Samui. Perhaps she was just letting us know her final stop. Resisting the need to involve myself, I decided to wait for a moment in case my advice was unwelcome. There were times when I tried so hard to help people that it was misplaced. Sometimes people don't need my help, but instead would rather possibly make a mistake and find their own way.

The girls exchanged a few more words, mentioning the full

moon party which Koh Pangnan was famous for, and then the travel plans unfolded more eloquently.

"So, I don't think I will still be there for the full moon party, but I'm not that bothered,"

"Yes, I am not too fussed, too many drunk people really," Jas replied. My head answered, 'I would definitely love to witness that, all the neon body paint, loud music and giving thanks for another full moon.' I loved the idea of worshipping things which we took for granted. Every so often I took a moment to thank the sun for coming up once again, and for the trees blooming. Each bee which buzzed past in the garden was a blessing too. Without such wonders of nature, where would we be? No earth to live on, and no books to produce. Since I was old enough to realise disasters happen, after the heartbreaking Bradford fire and the Hillsborough tragedy, I had appreciated the beauty of a peaceful nature. I was a young teenager at the time when I witnessed the horrific TV footage being shown. Without speaking, I took myself to the toilet. It was always cold in there, but I didn't notice the temperature. Closing the lilac painted door behind me, I leaned my back on it for a moment, like I had seen people do in the films. I gathered it would give me a chance to take a breath and recalibrate what had just happened. The biggest fear I had lived with until that point was my brother sitting on my legs and torturing me by tickling my feet. I tried to wriggle so frantically, lashing around, trying to get him off. All he did was laugh and carry on tickling. Mum just told us, "Pack it in you two," when I begged her to tell him to never do it again. My woeful worries seemed insignificant in comparison to those sporting tragedies. Shock remained with me for a long time after seeing those images of those supporters. It was a time when I began to know my inner fears were insignificant in comparison, and I had started to try and keep it under control. I wasn't sure I was doing a very good job at all.

There was the fear of the school bullies, but that was more pain than fear. I didn't sense I was in actual danger from them, I was simply being hurt by their cruelty. I still don't know why they suddenly yelled across the science lab, announcing my lesbianism, after they were best friends with me the day before. It had been the shock of my life at that time, to realise people who you trusted to be your friends could suddenly make up something which wasn't true and turn your life upside down. Over the years, I had worked hard on keeping the concern of that happening again at bay, but occasionally it crept up on me. People seemed to hurt me over and over and I just wanted to shower everyone with love and care. It was a curse.

Seeing those people lose their lives in front of our eyes, I realised that sometimes bad things happened on a very large scale. Anxiety showed its face slightly, but I had no clue that was a thing. My intrusive thoughts were something I believed everyone lived with. Before long, I was settled back into a life of worry about being sat on by my brother, and the school bullies turning the final four people in the school year against me, to make a complete pack. I never took the big stuff for granted again. The moon, in all its glory, may have been an excuse for the people visiting Koh Pangnan to have a good drinking session, but I decided to interpret it into giving thanks for the world turning and the moon spinning. Wait, did the moon spin? My endeavours to keep life as simple as that were a total failure, as I continued to think about living life in the very best way possible. Figuring that out in my head was another wonder of the world.

"Yeah, well, there will definitely be drink but I need to figure how to get there first. My friend lives there at the moment and she said I need to fly into Koh Samui and then," the conversation continued as the driver came in to nod at us. It was time to go. On the bus, the new friend told Jasmine how her friend was one half of a couple who decided to live on Koh Pangnan for a while as her boyfriend was doing PhD research, which he could do from anywhere in the world. My ears switched on. My PhD was still on hold and I had no idea if I might be likely to get back to it. My research area felt more defunked now that Covid was kind of over, and after being told for the third time how frustrated my supervisor was with me, I crumbled.

The conversation was so interesting, and it showed me just how many people were waking up to living a life like this. Move somewhere, work from there, enjoy the surroundings, do what you love. People still clocking in and out each day, hustling, toiling and listening to bosses being frustrated at them might be ok for some people, but it wasn't ok for me. I had no idea how apparent that would become.

5

An airport like no other

We both smiled as we looked out of the plane window. Below us there were glimmers of gold in the shape of the big Buddha and the jolly Buddha next to it.

"Wow, look, there they are," Jasmine pointed. We had seen these figures over and over as we researched Koh Samui, and now we saw them for real. Why did seeing things in front of you feel so different to seeing it on TV? I wondered if that was an entire research project in itself, the phenomenology of seeing iconic figures.

As soon as we landed, the plane was surrounded by little golf carts to carry the people to the terminal building. They were painted blue and had adverts of the local tourist attractions on them. Once again, these sights were familiar after seeing the buggies on YouTube, but I was overjoyed to see them in front of us.

"Oh Jas."

The Irish girl walked past us, and we didn't exchange words again verbally. In my mind I wished her the very best time of her life. I was so excited for her to be experiencing all the things she was about to see. She arrived in the terminal building before us, as we hung back to be the last people on the vehicles, so we could vlog, take selfies, and lap up the moment. My face was alive on those photos. My dimples were slightly deeper than usual, and I wasn't afraid to show my imperfect teeth. It reminded me of the home movies I had recently put on to digital back when I had a twinkle in my eyes.

Watching the footage back, I saw those little children who were my twins at almost two years old. I whispered, 'oh there they are,' which may seem strange to some. But even though I see my children every day, they are different children now. Back then, they were a type of human, and now they are a different type of human. They made me happy then, and I was happy with them now. But I missed them. I missed that happy time. We were so poor. We had no money for healthy food and could just about pay the bills. Dad helped me pay for my car, which I was sure I would have to sell when I first fell pregnant. That was a time before I realised life wasn't designed to be so awful. I just believed things like that happened and saw no reason to question it. The language I had been programmed with were the typical phrases that we now know we must avoid.

'Money doesn't grow on trees.'

'That's just our kind of luck.'

Knowing life can be different, and trying to undo that programme is a beast. It's like fighting against the wind. You know you can do it, but it takes so much effort.

Kev was in my life back then and occasionally he would take the camera and turn it on to me. He was holding the camera and I was looking over the lens at him, I looked different. Maybe because he held the camera, and I thought I loved him, I had a spark in my eyes and the similar look that I had on the golf cart. As I watched back that old footage, I clasped my lips with my hand. I was shocked. Who was she? Where was she? Could I get her back again or had life done some permanent damage?

Even if it was temporary, she was here, on this tarmac, in Koh Samui.

As we walked into the airport to collect our luggage, we headed to something which looked as if it was passport control. The buildings were all outside really, with thatches for rooves, and cascading leaves from above. I watched as people in front of us collected their passports from their hand luggage and handed them over.

"Ah, thank you." I was sure I saw a smile from the person checking the passport. Something unusual felt as if it was stirring inside of me. This was already so unique. A smile at passport control, and a thank you, in contrast to the usual nod and grunt you would get from someone behind the glass. Did they usually try to intimidate you so you would behave increasingly better? That didn't usually turn out too well. Instead, that behaviour created monsters with backpacks on, including me. Travel could be stressful. Always, travel was worth the pain it took to get there, otherwise I had to guess we wouldn't go in the first place. Even though the trip to Asia had excited me more than any other, I knew it would be a white-knuckle ride full of various cultures and plane rides.

The heat carried some kind of smell into my nostrils as I realised, we would have to sharpen up the way we dressed. The sweat kept coming out of the pores and soaking our clothes. Part of me was happy about the heat, another part was uncomfortable. My fingertips moved my fringe away from my forehead and the wet trickled down my fingers. I could almost sense the salt in my mouth. I made a mental note to keep drinking water.

Very soon it was time for us two blonde tourists to move forwards to the window, and have our passports stamped. My joints were fluid, I was happy, we moved forwards. I moved my eyes from looking at the floor ahead and drew a line up to a little lady in front of me.

"Hello," I said. She nodded her head slowly at me. Looking down at the passports, she muttered a word I didn't know yet. I would learn a few words if I could, just to ensure I didn't seem typically ignorant.

Thud! Thud! The stamp planted ink into a well-used page in my passport, among the other reminders of countries we had visited.

On the other side of the passport hut was a large, vaulted ceiling. Daylight shone over the pillars holding the roof up. I expected there would be many spiders up there. Dark mahogany coloured wood created this building which was housed here to protect the belt where the suitcases would arrive. We had previously seen a screen with the number 1 on it and our departure airport next to that, just so we could tell which carousel our suitcases would be on. Jasmine glanced at me sideways and her mouth illuminated into a smile.

"There's only one," she said. She looked like a little explorer who was much younger than her actual age of 24 years. Her backpack sat elegantly on her back as she leaned down to collect the bag which she spotted. The baby pink hard case, with handles on the sides for ease, was Jasmines. Mine was black, and a little bit manly. Aqua blue straps created a Criss cross for safety and aesthetics, although a few dark marks had been picked up along the way. Cases with scars always seemed fascinating.

Once we had both suitcases, we tried to leave the building, which was actually just a lid on a piece of outside, but it was difficult to move quickly in this quirky building as we feasted on the visual delights. Lotus flowers sat among lilies in a pond which separated the next building from the taxi drivers. There was very little chaos, just busy. And that was a different feeling totally. Next to the lily pond was a blue sign planted into the ground. The sign was waist height. A backdrop of green and red plants and leaves were spiking towards the sign highlighted the letters which spelt 'Samui Airport'. Taking my phone out of my cross body black and white bag, I reached up high to take a selfie. The angle always made me look my best; younger, with less double chin.

"Come on," I called to Jasmine and she stood behind me and peered over my shoulder. She smiled so widely her teeth glowed.

Red cheeks, from the heat, we were glowing. I snapped the shot right before we wandered into the toilets, which were strangely air conditioned.

"So already, my hair is ruined, it's just so humid, but it doesn't matter because it's perfect, perfect, perfect and I can't wait to explore this tropical place. It just looks amazing." I vlogged to the camera and the joy in my face didn't need to be animated for the sake of the camera, I was delighted.

One of the autumn evenings when we sat at the dining room table, I said I felt this would be the trip of a lifetime. We had notebooks, credit cards and pens surrounding us as we searched on the internet to find as many good deals as we could and aimed to figure an itinerary for ourselves.

"Mum don't say that. Don't put that kind of pressure on it. It might not be. And once you've said it, you've attached to it." She wasn't wrong. But I wanted our Asia trip to be wonderful, when I turned 50, just before Covid was invented, we went to Mexico. I saved a lot of money from my remortgage to spend on a trip for the twins and I, to celebrate turning fifty. The travel agent had assured me that the best value for money she had ever spent was in Mexico. After I googled, long stretches of white sand popped onto my screen and I was sold. £5k later and we were booked.

Travel often made me grumpy. My AS caused a lot of pain and it was not easy to be jolly and feel uncomfortable and shattered at the same time. I remember speaking to Julie on voice note from Playa del Carmen, right after a refreshing downpour had ended and the sun created steam on the pathways.

'We had to walk so far, and the golf buggies drove past really fast. We called out to them, but they just ignored us, then another one went past and that guy looked at me and sneered and shook his head when I called for a second time. When we want to come to sit by the pool its like 10,000 steps. Crazy that they have bus stops in the resort. It's that huge. Anyway, how are you?' I clicked send. A short while later, she replied.

'Oh, my, god.' She started speaking slowly, as if she was unable to comprehend something, 'you are there in paradise and still someone can be unhappy. It just shows you; it doesn't matter what, you can be unhappy.' I felt judged, even though she had tried to contain her voice so that it didn't sound as if she was talking about me. I hadn't quite learned about myself enough to realise my mood was affected by the prodding of a needle over and over into the small of my back. Irritation. Even though I accept my pain more now, and I realise it is just a part of who I am, rather like my occasional grumpiness, I am the person who is most affected by that, and learning to live with that mood is the best thing I have ever done for myself. The day Julie decided I was too irritating to deal with anymore was a day I let go of attachments to hoping people would be there to love you for the rest of your life. It's true what they say, people come for seasons and they go again. I try not to be annoying, but I also try to think sometimes, it's not always my fault. One thing I didn't want to do was annoy my darling daughter with my positive expectations of our trip to Asia together. I kept a lid on my excitement leading up to the trip. Pressure cookers had less at stake than me, as I suspected I would be in pain, anxious and tired. I wanted to be excited for the travelling we were about to begin. What if it was disappointing? If life didn't bring things to really look forward to, was there any point in continuing to live, when all it was giving me was pain and exhaustion? I had to keep excited about things. I knew the glass was half full on this beautiful earth and all I needed to do was find the thing to tap into that feeling and do more of that. I had been searching since I was taught by a wise book that life should not be a white-knuckle ride.

Inside the sliding doors of the toilet block was a wall full of underwater pictures. It was blue everywhere we looked as I was witnessing paradise in front of my eyes. The cold of the air conditioning was welcoming, and we used the bathroom area to prepare ourselves for the journey ahead. We didn't know how we would be travelling to the next destination.

We pulled our bags behind us as we headed to the exit of the airport.

A map of the island was ahead of us with cartoon animations of the various towns. Samui was a heart shaped island with a little unusual flick towards the left ventricle. New places always bring new geography to learn. I had booked Lamai as our choice of resort. Close to Chewang, the most popular beach and busiest place for parties, it was an accessible resort but far enough away from the main strip. Jasmine wouldn't have liked being on the strip.

My research was inaccurate, and Lamai was around 30

minute's drive from Chaweng, Fishermen's Village and the airport. Most of the activity was at the North of the island, and Lamai was kind of east, almost south east. Cab rides were easy to organise using a company called Grab, which we heard from YouTube was a little similar to Uber. I had never used Uber, as that was the kids' jobs. As a non-drinker, I drove everywhere and had never needed to use Uber. But I was prepared for this trip, I had Grab as an app, I had cash, and I had my sim card. So, we could get to wherever we wanted to go. A ride in a Grab taxi was only going to be equivalent to £3 to drive for half an hour. A strange concept to fathom, after the price hikes of everything in the UK. Things being affordable was a refreshing change, and I liked it.

After a short study of the map, and a quick photograph which was a smart marketing move by the airport, we moved forward. I looked at the screen of my phone. The photo looked ok really. I stood in front of a couple of angel wings which had the island name written across it. Their marketing team would have known that photo would end up on many people's Instagram. I looked at what I was wearing. Tight blue cycling shorts, which I had bought for my trip to Greece the year before when I was working on a contract out there. As my son took a photo of me in those shorts in Turkey the previous winter, the angle made me peachy. Such vanity over that photo saw me post it on Instagram. It was fake. I couldn't look like that with the naked eye, I was sure. Despite lifting at the gym most days, I felt sure those shorts just hiked up the blubber beneath. As they were tight, they helped against chaffing on these sweaty days. Hence, they were my choice. But to cover up the extra skin from having the twins, a huge white t-shirt covered most of the rest of my body. The pictures on the front of my t-shirt were cute and inspirational.

'Love yourself first'

'Heal the planet'

And huge flowers were hand drawn on the images. I felt safe in that t shirt, but I wasn't sure it was the most flattering thing to wear. Heat almost took away the need for high fashion, although Jas managed to look as darling as ever. I tutted at myself as I closed the image down and tucked my phone away into my bag. We continued to walk past the mahogany pillars which were encircled with pots three quarters of the way up. Cascading flowers draped over the edges of the pots and I was walking with my mouth half open. This airport was feeling like a trip into my mind. Rustic and beautiful, full of nature and beauty and realising that while details mattered, perfection didn't. Unlike Abu Dhabi, Unlike Heathrow Terminal 4. How could all of these airports be so different? All born from the same atoms, all featuring sequences like the next, but the difference was one thing: energy.

6

Lamai

"She will give you a price," the man pointed. He was keen to get us into his taxi. I looked over at the trail he created with his brown, wrinkled index finger and looked at the desk. The person he referred to was a transgender female. She was stunning. Her make up was applied perfectly and her features were symmetrical. She smiled at us as we approached. The taxi drivers' words echoed for a few moments in my head and I admired how easily he called the woman 'she'. Readily accepted in Thailand, this set me at ease. People who judged me for being me wouldn't understand how settling it was to feel part of an inclusive environment; however that looked.

The usual yelling was absent. The dust which often accompanied the pollution of an underground car park escaped as there was no underground. It was a small airport, but there was a lot going on once a plane had landed. But there was no shouting, no irritations at each other. If someone called out to a taxi driver, the tone was elevated to carry the voice across the airwaves but there was no screaming. No whistles blew. There were no police. This was most unusual.

"Going to Lamai, how much please," I asked the lady. She pulled up a red sign which listed prices for taxis.

"600, it's 600," she pointed to the area on the sign which showed where we were going and the listed price of 600. This showed us that we wouldn't be bartering. A quick calculation was needed so we could know we were not going to be spending our entire sum of money, and we realised this trip was going to cost around £12.92, which seemed reasonable. It would cost the same from my local train station to home which is only three miles.

I nodded towards the taxi driver and he pointed back to the lady who was asking for payment there. This was civilised and I felt as though no one could feel violated with the costs. I liked it.

On an airport transfer, my phone was only used to take photos, no browsing.

"You love a transfer, Mum," Jasmine grinned as we fastened our seatbelts. I smiled back at her and my excitement gave my face a glow.

As I watched green plants whizz past the taxi window, I realised this place was exactly as I had imagined, even though I had not imagined the streets and this drive. After watching so much content about Bali, this is how I had imagined Bali.

Ubud was not so far away, when you look at the globe. It was also high on my list of places to visit, just as Uluwatu was. I wanted to sit on bean bags and watch the sunset by a beach bar which fuelled my soul with gentle vibes. Koh Samui was hitting all those spots from what I could see so far.

Would I be able to find some peace on this island?

Would this be the place I could finally be the real me?

7

Zara Beach

The taxi turned underneath a chaotic load of comms cables ahead, and past a gym labelled up 'Perfect Bodies,' before we took a side street.

"We must be here Jas," I said to my daughter who was enjoying a scroll on her phone.

"Ohh," she sat up higher in her chair and looked out of the window. We drove past some houses which would have been declared derelict back home. They had great character. A lady with a pointed hat was gardening, with a cardigan on. She pulled her hoe upright and leaned on it with one hand and placed the other hand on her hip. She stood up and looked out at the garden. I wondered what she thought.

In front of us was a blank horizon, which always meant you were near the sea. After a few more yards of driving, the taxi reached the end of the road. To our left there was an entrance which looked just like Bali, with two grey stone pillars and a sign announcing Zara Beach.

"Zara Beach," I said beneath my breath. Ahead of us was a path leading to the resort we were about to call home for the next few days. I wondered if our stay was too brief and took my gaze back to the entrance. Jasmine checked that we didn't owe the driver any more money and we both stepped out of the car. A single sunbeam shone through the trees and over the top of the roof which housed the reception desk. No doors or walls were around the reception and I figured this was the most bizarre hotel entrance I had ever seen. Rain covers, that seemed to be all that was needed in this country. No windows or walls for most of the buildings. An open wooden gate was fixed to black painted wooden posts and white concrete posts almost enclosed the reception in. Above the concrete was a single sign on the right-hand side which said 'Zara Beach resort Lamai Koh Samui,' and each of those words were in a different font. I had never seen the font which said Zara before, but it looked rustic, and I liked it. Above the pointed reception roof were lush green trees and to one side was a tree which I would have referred to as a palm tree. I was soon to learn these were coconut trees and they were full of the droops, which is the name for the fruit of a coconut tree. It isn't actually a nut, or some fruit, it's a droop. I learned that during my nutrition degree. A coconut is full of goodness; and antimicrobial, anti-bacterial and a fabulous food for the microbiota, I knew this place was going to be good for my body and soul. Excitement saw my dimples alive once again, and we drank in the sights ahead of us as we started to consider hauling our heavy suitcases up four concrete steps towards the reception desk.

"Hello. Usher?"

"Yes," Jasmine replied, we both raised our eyebrows. We

were earlier than any hotel could cater for, as that was the only time we could get our flight, but it was also the most incredible place to be for as long as possible. I already knew that, but a strong endorsement was soon to embrace me.

On each side of the reception desk was a bamboo arrangement. Was it real? Probably. Sofa type of chairs were made from some form of branches, and while they didn't look as if you could sleep on them, they added to the stunning aesthetic of this reception area.

Jasmine, being a strong little, tiny thing, lugged our cases one at a time up the steps to the reception desk as we were met by a brown skinned man with wide shoulders and a welcoming smile. To his side was a small, younger man dressed in pink, with a cross body bag. The two of them exchanged some words which seemed as calm at the Samui sea, and the younger man rushed to help Jasmine with the bags.

Settling near the swimming pool, which was much smaller than we were used to, we cradled our hand luggage beside us for safety and ordered some cold drinks. A glass made of thin opaque material, cloudy ice cubes and a slice of something zesty arrived and the barman poured a drink for me and Jasmine. It didn't occur to us to embrace the speed of the ice melting, and instead we meandered with different camera angles as we took enough photos to be able to celebrate the start of this holiday.

Wiping away the droplets of salty fluid from the top of my lip, I took a sip of my favourite drink and swallowed. I smiled. I looked to my right at my stunning daughter who was sat beside me on a Bali bed. We decided to share the Bali bed for a while and just sit for a moment while we tried to embrace the heat, the vibe, the island life. Surreal discussions swam in my head as I felt comfortable with my body and my mind. Seldom was this the case in my life, but I was so grateful.

"Cute little pool," I nodded.

"Sweet isn't it."

"Looks a little bit like an um, water feature," we both laughed and decided to finish our drinks, put our backpacks over our shoulders and venture out a little. Sandy shores were whispering to me in the rhythm of the sea, and I couldn't resist but to run to this adventure with my arms open.

8

Being

There was nowhere else I would rather have been than to sit at the plastic table, with the red chequered tablecloth, with sand under my toes.

I couldn't find any words as I observed the serenity of the sea. It didn't occur to me to mind that there was a fried fly in our triple cooked chips. We stopped eating them as soon as we saw it, but prior to that we had enjoyed the oil laden fries which took the edge off needing any real food to eat. The best iced coffee was giving me even more reasons to fall in love with this island.

High hopes were a worry before we landed on Koh Samui.

"I'm just going for another paddle, is that ok?" Jasmine nodded to give me consent as she knew as well as I did that the sea was as warm as a bath and very enticing. People had mentioned in the past, 'the sea is as warm as a bath,' and we just nodded knowing that meant the sea was not freezing. This sea on Koh Samui was as warm as a lukewarm bath.

Stepping on the soft sand, my toes burrowed into the white powder as I made my way towards the water. The next time Jasmine looked up, I waved at her and grinned. I gestured in sign language, mimicking charades, to indicate that she should film. I found myself entranced by the sea, submerged up to my neck in its allure. How could I be any happier than this?

Torn between wanting to float in the sea and fancying drinking my coffee, I grinned at my quiet mind. This feeling of freedom and peace was something I would need to start getting used to over the next few days. Time to think, time to breathe properly, time to succumb to the elements surrounding my skin. Time to just be.

Hours passed as we sat at the table. We watched a man cutting back the roots of a tree with his hands. He didn't need any tools. He casually tossed an unripe coconut to one side. Life was very different on this island. I had added an affirmation with 'island life' on my vision board, some years ago. If there was ever a place to answer my call to feel an island vibe, this was it. After we finished our drinks, Jasmine and I began a slow-paced walk along the beach, away from our hotel. Time was a vacant option; it didn't matter. My backpack was heavy, even though I had left my laptop at home, on the other side of the world. We continued to walk.

"Is that the rocks? You know, Grandpa rocks?" Jasmine asked as the shielded her eyes with a flat hand. I looked at the horizon and noticed some light grey rocks perched at the edge of the sea. Had they fallen from a cliff? I wasn't sure of the true story, but I did wonder if she was right. Was that Hin Ta and Hin Yai?

Blue skies merged into the lighter blue shades of the sea and highlighted the outer edges of the grey rocks. I tried to squint and see the outline of the shapes of the rocks. My research had given me the perplexing knowledge of these rocks, which were a distinct landmark of Lamai. According to local folklore, the rocks represented an old couple, Ta Kreng (Grandfather Kreng) and Yai Riem (Grandmother Riem), who were shipwrecked off the coast of Koh Samui. The lovers morphed into these rocks as a testament to their love and fidelity, and as a message to their would-be in-laws about their intentions to arrange a marriage for their son. While a part of me loved the romance of this folklore, I also realised that people flocked every day to look at a bunch of geology which was said to represent male and female geniatalia. Made of granite and naturally sculpted over time by the elements, the peculiar shapes were the result of erosion and weathering, which had given them their unique and suggestive appearances. Curiosity and humour brought tourists to these rocks to take photos and to stare at the Hin Ta Grandfather rock in its upright phallic symbol. Next to Hin Ta, the Grandmother rock, Hin Yai had a horizontal resemblance to female genitals. I understood while people would go and see this spectacle, but already I was falling in love with the beautiful beach, lush landscape and warm welcomes of this island, and I hoped people would see more than just some sexy stones.

My eyes needed a telescope to see for sure if those were the famed rocks, and I decided to wait until the following day to see them close up, on our tour of the island. Instead, I snuggled back into the relaxed and happy feeling which was being cradled from the sensation of soft sand and warm sea beneath my feet. I looked down at my pale pink toenails and saw some occasional empty shells sprinkled in the perfect shoreline. My eyes trailed upwards to see what lied just in front of me. Instantly I stopped. I grabbed Jasmine's arm to the right of me. I cupped my mouth with my hand. I inhaled to speak.

"Oh look, Oh Jas."

"aww," she replied. Ahead of us were two little dogs playing in the sand. Their coats were soggy, and sand clumped together in thick strands under their bellies. Little whispers of joy escaped their chops. I stood still. I stared at the dogs. One of them was white in colour and looked like a cross breed. The other dog was probably a cross too but the markings on this dog were close enough to be almost identical to our little Harley. My heart still hurt. Was this a sign from spirit to say hello? Was he wishing us a nice time and telling us to enjoy this paradise? I didn't know what the reason for seeing these dogs, but I was reminded of a time when life felt perfect. Sitting with Harley, writing, in a coffee shop, was my idea of the perfect working day. I would take a few snacks for him in a clip pot, and another small clip pot to pour some fresh water in to. He would never drink from dog bowls. He was a fussy dog. Yet he never complained when he was cold, so I learned to keep an eye on his shivers and wrapped a blanket around him. Sometimes we would sit there for hours on end, and he would snuggle into my leg until it was time to go outside for a sniff and to mark his territory. Those were the best days. Leaving him at home while I went to work from the library, or somewhere I couldn't take him, was heartbreaking, especially as I knew time was limited. He and I would appreciate life was as good as it would ever get in those moments. People wouldn't appreciate that I was working. They would just see it was me sitting in a coffee shop, having the luxury of free time. In fact, this was me hoping to live a life I had dreamed of. This was my writing time, this was the time I would get to create, in the hope that I could help other people.

Living though such dramatic stories had to have a point to it. Otherwise, what was the lesson from it? I felt sure I could just help others to live a better life by realising that these ups and downs were inevitable and we would all be okay, if we just kept the faith. It felt like my reason for being, it felt like my purpose. People may argue we don't have a purpose, and we should just meander through life and take the good with the bad. But my belief of helping to heal the planet and starting with helping others to feel better, was a strong believe, as strong as those rocks which faced the elements. Yet Harley and I would leave the coffee shop and let life get in the way once again, while demands of paying bills, looking after children and ageing parents, and keeping the bathroom clean enough not to appease an OCD boyfriend, stopped this life as a writer. When life got out of the way in 2020, there was space to write a best seller or two. I needed life to be out of the way just enough to embrace this feeling of joy which occasionally drifted in to create the best version of me.

59

9

Bliss

Looking back over my time on earth so far, 2020 was my favourite. Negatives aside, this was a time when I didn't notice the ticking clock. I sat at my desk for fourteen hours a day, exchanging emails back and forth and gathering stories from other people. Putting the anthology together for long periods of the day was bliss. Joy streamed through my inner self. Walking in woods which we hadn't ever discovered before, also brought a smile to my face. My son would use the fallen trees to continue his power lifting training and occasionally he would use his twin sister to add to the weight. We spent time being human. And the other stuff stopped getting in the way of being simply human for a while.

I have known since I was a child that my happy times are the moments when I have a pen and paper in my hands. Now those hands are less photogenic, yet my words are more powerful, and finding a place to label those words has been so difficult. This inner knowing of my plea in the world can feel torturous at times. A film called 'Yesterday' told a story of the Beatles, and the phenomena of them vanishing, having never been. The main character visited John

Lennon as an old man, who resided alone in a shack of a home on the edge of the water on an island in, what looked like, Scotland. John painted pictures to while away his time. Nothing like Pablo Picasso, these canvases were something to please John, while he lived in his simple home, with a simple stack of mugs on a shelf, and clearly with little money.

When the visitor asked, "are you happy, John?" he was met with a quizzical expression.

"Happy? Erm, yeah I guess so," John replied, as if it was never something to be aimed for. He was simply being. The old John had possibly never reached for the stars, hoping for more. He was peaceful.

Another book I read had highlighted the experience of living with a musical genius. Sometimes, sitting at the dinner table, inspiration would strike, and the musician would leave the table to go and write. He likened it to an irritation, living with that gift. I understood the sentiment. It's like, something inside of you keeps tap-tap-tapping until you listen. Then you listen and do a little bit of what it needs. Then life gets in the way, and you hear humans around you telling you to stop dreaming, to get a job, to pay the mortgage, to live a life of burying your bliss.

Inside, I would scream, 'no!'

I lost friends, I faced criticism; people thought I was strange. I don't disagree with them. I was never the person at school who followed the crowd. Even at work, I would try and make things better, feel better, encourage a path of least resistance. But the minute you surrounded yourself with those humans again, they convinced you that your way was the resistance, not the flow.

Dad gave up his bliss to follow the path of least resistance when he knew that Mum was going to make his life as difficult as she could. There were threats, and I was just a baby, but I can imagine Dad surrendering, and realising that the life of joy was not going to occur in this human time. I know he is at peace now, and when people ask if I wish he was still here, I tell them no. Dealing with Mum now would just cause him more torment; he had enough.

Giving up my bliss was an idea I fooled around with on many occasions. Life threw paths in the way to stop me carving out the time to write. Other times it forced me to think that writing was the only way. Not once did I consider not writing, even if it was journalling each day.

Every morning, I would wake and move into a different wave of brain state. Then the smile would appear; it was time to write. The kettle would boil, I would make coffee, I would choose a pen and I would pour some words onto a page with no agenda, other than to please the inner self which was calling out to me. Some days, I would have more time than others. Some days, I had to go and earn some money. Some days, I would wonder if I could write and earn money. Others had done that, perhaps I could too.

Writing feels fresh to me. There was never any challenge about not writing. I had to write.

2013 was the year I realised I might need to start heading towards a future after the children had left home. I was newly divorced, and my ex and I discussed ideas. Another passion I had always pursued was food and nutrition. This was in a realm I considered 'work' as it was something I was successful at and got paid well for. It was my job. I decided to formalise my science qualification and potentially help people with health issues who needed nutrition and lifestyle advice. Nutrition was in its infancy and people were not listening.

I struggled through my science degree and at the end of it, I had a clear direction. I wanted to speak to people who had improved their health with nutrition, diet, lifestyle and give a holistic account of how other people could do this. I wanted to gather stories of people with chronic disease and inspire others with the stories of better health. My cohort were confused when I announced I was going to do a MA in Creative Non-Fiction writing.

"How does that work then?" the scientists asked me. To me, it was obvious. Yes, it was interdisciplinary, and it was cross faculty, but I knew I could make a success of being a writer, and a nutritionist. I had the knowledge to self-publish and I flew myself to Bosnia and Herzegovina during my MA, to figure out my direction. I spent time exploring, with my friends who were hosting me, and spent the rest of the time pitching to agents to get my work published with one of the big five. I listened within as I was in the shower on my fourth morning in Bosnia. This felt wrong.

Learning how to self-publish was an emerging route, and I created a community of others who had successfully taken the same route. I made my firm decision and continued to gather stories to publish. Boxes were being ticked. I felt content and hopeful.

Why did I stare at these rocks, knowing a trip like this was once in a lifetime? Why didn't I have enough money to pay the bills and buy food? Was I falling into the trap of the cost of living, like many others? It was real. It was difficult. Could the answer be provided in the digital world of writing? Surely there was a better way? I knew a way which felt better, and that was writing. I didn't want it to have to add a price tag to it, as the importance of this work was to help people, not to have to pay my bills. This was art.

Previously, I could have drunk more coffee, stayed up late or woken naturally at 4am, fuelled by worry and stress hormones. Sleep was important now that I was feeling slightly older and staying up writing until 2am after a full day of work, caring for mum and keeping a nice house was impossible.

The folklore of the Hin Yai Hin Ta rocks gave me a warm feeling. There was another myth I had learned about in Banja Luka, which David had explained to me. A story of love, loyalty and tragedy.

"Meet Safikada, a young and beautiful woman whose fate was forever entwined with the walls of the Kastel Fortress in the city. Her heart knew no boundaries when she fell in love with a handsome Austro-Hungarian soldier.

Fraternising with these occupying troops was forbidden. Nevertheless, their love blossomed. Fate had other plans—a sudden order sent him away, leaving their happiness unfulfilled.

Safikada and her soldier made a solemn promise: eternal love and loyalty until the grave.

So, when news of his death on the battlefield arrived in Banja Luka her world was shattered.

Desperate and heartbroken, Safikada stood before the cannon that marked noon firing from the Kastel, declaring, "I am loyal to you until the grave."

Her lifeless body fell where today's monument stands—a place where lovers still light candles for their own (un)happy loves."

There was something magical about hearing such stories: myths, legends, folklore or truth.

"If you follow your bliss, you put yourself on a kind of track that has been there all the while, waiting for you, and the life that you ought to be living is the one you are living. Wherever you are – if you are following your bliss, you are enjoying that refreshment, that life within you, all the time." Joseph Campbell, who speaks of the hero's journey, covered many aspects of the human experience. While he discusses the theory of the archetypal hero, his philosophy of 'follow your bliss' has lent itself to influence many stories over many years. His work gained much momentum after he died, and I wondered if my work was heading in the same direction. I had no hesitation that it was important to tell the stories of others, but would it be in my lifetime, or after it? I was afraid of it being too hot to handle, as I was afraid of everything. But as I understand more about Campbell, it sounds as though none of this is a choice. It's as if this is not our business. We are put on the earth for a reason, and it will unfold in its own sweet time.

As I began my PhD journey, I knew I wanted to look at the human experience and the deeper meaning of it. I stumbled upon, or downloaded, a concept named phenomenology which seemed to be a natural understanding to me which was made more complex than it needed to be. Feed in some anthropology, which is kind of what I enjoy, the study of humans and the behaviour of people and their belief systems, and who can begin to argue. We believe what we believe, and it serves us, or it doesn't. Hermeneutics is another player in the words which try to explain what I love. But at the end of the day, if I listened within, I loved people and their stories. I wanted to help make sense of the world through other people and their stories. Sometimes some other words, Ethnography or Biography were added in to the recipe which made up the confused description when people said, 'what do you do?' I would always begin with,

"Well, it's difficult to explain quickly," when I wished I would just answer, "I am a writer," which is a statement feels like following my bliss.

10

Check in

Seconds became minutes, which became immeasurable, full moments of floating along the shore towards the rocks and then back again. Our hand luggage was full of important documents and we took the weight of our necessary goods on our shoulders in our back packs. We knew it would be time to check in soon and there was a void of any great emotion about that. Sometimes, on an all-inclusive trip, all there really is to aim for is the hotel grounds, the welcome drink, and dinner times. Here, this beach was a total pageant winner when it came to claiming our attention. The sand was enchanting and while the hotel also seemed like a magical place, there was no great preference. I was delighted to be sensing our surroundings and time seemed as invisible as it actually was.

Heading towards the reception of Zara beach, we walked as if we were floating.

"Hello, ah, yes, we are ready for you, just here," the reception manager looked on the desk, lifting pieces of A4 paper. We just stood, no hurry, just waiting.

Three minutes passed, breeze blew the greenery around us

and I smiled at the tree above the reception roof. I thought it was a coconut tree, but I was not well versed enough in this little island yet to be sure. I hoped to learn more as I called this wonderful place home for the next few nights. The idea behind staying in Koh Samui was simply to ensure we had no jet lag when it was the championship day. Jet lag was absent so far. I seemed to be thankful for every little thing on this journey so far. I was happy.

The reception manager took us to a set of concrete steps at the side of his desk and his colleague helped carry Jasmine's case. I walked down the steps too slowly, for fear of falling and we ventured through a doorway opening which housed no door. In front of us were paving slabs which were dotted here and there, at angles with the ground below. Trees outlined their roots in a bold, fantasy fashion as if fairies lived there. What was the story there? They were draped with vines and some of the leaves looked as large as me, as if they were from a banana tree. We passed a villa on our left, which had a small swimming pool outside. The roof had the same style of leaves draping just over the edge of the veranda. Wooden sun loungers sat sleepily on the side of the deck by the pool. This hotel was quaint and rustic; a little imperfect.

"When I booked this place, I was hoping for something different from all-inclusive hotel, something rustic and kind of island-y," I told the camera, "and boy did I get it."

Underneath the cascading trees, we walked with our bags, following the two local men. Concrete guards were at the entrance to the pathway towards our rooms. The villas were close enough to each other to feel cosy, but plenty of space for privacy. This was unique, and I was embraced by the nature sounds which I would have described as a rain forest in Australia. After a couple of minutes, we climbed two stairs. A green dipping pool was to our left, and newly scattered leaves had landed on top of the water, next to the villa. A single wooden sun lounger sat there, overlooking the pool.

"They are coming to clean soon," the man pointed at the pool; and I took no notice of his words. It didn't look particularly frequently cleaned, but I was wrong, a small man came along a few minutes after the announcement and took out the leaves and checked the chemicals in the pool. Every day, they cleaned the dipping pool. It was safe for human use.

Our guide stood above us, hoping to fit the key into the lock. He perched on the veranda. The space in front of me filled my eyes with delight. I could imagine sitting there, writing, with a coffee each morning. Beyond the veranda was a large, open field which looked like no man's land. This was perfect for the wildlife to reside in and give me a song full of their exclusive, indescribable sounds each day. Delight crept across my face like the sun rising from slumber.

"Here," the manager said as he handed us a key with a huge, wooden tab attached to it. The words "Zara Beach" looked as if they were burnt into the tab. He stepped inside the property and Jasmine followed him, then I was next. The vaulted ceilings were just as I had imagined, and I was sure this was the exact same property which I had seen vlogged on YouTube when I was researching the place. I remembered the vlogger wasn't overly enthusiastic about the accommodation which fascinated me as I likened it to some over water bungalow in the Maldives. But I wanted rustic and I wanted island. And this was it,

"Ohh look it's erm," I looked at an artistic photo of a model smoking. The picture was in black and white and occupied most of the far wall, above the brown leather sofa. I tried to remember the name of the famous model. I wondered why I felt the need to comment on a picture, when all of this exploring of such a beauty home was patiently waiting. Jasmine filled in the blanks with the models name, and I walked in and put my backpack on the floor inside of the entrance. My lips parted as I began to gaze at the house. This looked outstanding.

"I'll put this here, next to this," the man said as he laid the giant key fob next to the instruction manual which was also likened to burnt words on a wooden tab, and he left us to wander around our perfect new home.

11

Home

Under the vaulted ceilings, there was the most unusual shower room I had seen. The entire shower tray was made of grey concrete and it took up the entire floor space of the wet room, which was the size of a small bedroom. There were steps down to the floor, which was the depth of my leg, right up to my top of my quads. Such a strange shower, but I loved it. There were no windows, just fly nets, and they would have towered above your head as you showered to ensure dignity remained intact.

"Well, that's the strangest shower I have seen. But I like it,"

"Oh really Mum, let's see," Jasmine popped her head over my shoulder to see, "and you want to see this sink."

I turned to look behind Jasmine and there was a basin shaped like a plant pot, and it was huge. I fathomed it would be a good way to do the washing by hand at least. There were some water mark stains at the bottom of the basin, and there were angled glass shelves to either side of the basin, looking as if they needed to be fixed. I felt zero percent disappointment Nothing was making me feel negative.

The middle of the room was occupied with the usual brown,

wooden wardrobe with a safe, and iron and a few coat hangers inside; the reverse of this furniture island area was covered in floor to ceiling mirrors. The architect must have had some fun designing these houses.

Reflecting in the mirrors on the bed behind me were images of natural leaves and petals which had been gathered from outside. They were arranged to spell 'welcome' and the little flowers had hues of yellow towards the stems. I had never seen real versions of this flower. This was paradise.

Topping off the joy of our new home was a large bed, which I gave the knuckle test to. It felt incredible and I was later delighted to feel the sheets on my skin, which were even more wonderful than I imagined. The bed was paradise just as the island was.

"I wonder if we can get any more sun loungers?" Jas asked. There was only one, and I was sure we would be spending some time lying there, next to our villa, enjoying the sun and dipping in the pool.

"Surely," I said and took a breath. "Shall we get settled and go for a wander? Are you hungry?"

"A bit, yeah."

"Let me grab a coffee and write for a bit, see if I can get a sun lounger and you can unpack?"

Jasmine liked the idea that I wasn't wandering around waiting for her, so I left to see if I could find a coffee at the bar. My notebook and pen were in my bag and I was excited to get something onto the paper.

The sun filtered through the leaves, casting dappled light across the hotel's poolside. Koh Samui wrapped itself around me, its warm breezes and the distant murmur of waves calming my restless mind. I was here, thousands of miles from my everyday life, hoping to gather my thoughts and finally put something down on paper that felt real. But somehow, the words just wouldn't come.

I sat there, notebook open, staring at half-hearted scribbles that seemed to go nowhere. Out of the corner of my eye, I noticed a hoody was thrown onto the chair next to me. As the server brought my cappuccino in a glass cup, someone was settling into the lounge chair next to mine. Turning, my head, I did a double take, not quite believing it was him. The voice of a generation, a man who had sold out stadiums across the world. And here he was, just as much a guest in this little piece of paradise as I was.

I didn't stare, but it was impossible not to steal glances. After a while, he caught my eye and gave a faint smile.

"Good place to think, isn't it?" he said, nodding toward my notebook.
I laughed, feeling a little embarrassed.

"Yea, maybe too good. It's hard to get much written when it's this relaxing."
He leaned back in his chair, gazing out at the pool's rippling water. "I get that. I came here for the same reason; needed a break from the madness." His tone was casual, but it felt surreal to be having a conversation with someone so famously out of reach.

We began talking. I found myself opening up, admitting how

I'd been struggling to write, how I wasn't even sure I was on the right path.

"Do you fancy talking more about this? I have to head back, just, because, but you are welcome to sit. There's something I would love to share," he meant nothing flirtatious, and I had no reason to say no. I nodded and smiled as I began to gather my things.

As we walked past the bar, I looked at the staff, "oh, I almost forgot, can we please have another sun lounger? We only have one by the pool."

On our way to check in, Jas and I had walked past the most luxurious looking place, and there was a guy in the pool, just laying, with his head leaning back. I decided in that moment he had the best villa. I didn't know it was Simon. As he turned up the steps, I gasped and held my mouth. "This is the most stunning villa in Zara Beach right?"

"It is isn't it. I come here when I can. It's such an escape. Love it." His blue eyes pierced into me. I wanted the option to be able to take my creative brain somewhere to work on my craft. He let out a little grin as if he could see exactly what I was feeling.

"Coke is it?" He had noticed my drink from by the bar. I nodded and he gave a sign for me to sit by the pool. As he walked away, I tried to see inside the villa but it gave similar hues to the one we were staying in. As Simon returned, he looked at me and quirkily laughed, just like I'd seen him do on Instagram, handing me a glass with ice and a can of Coke.

"Ok, now talk."

"I've always been a writer," I confessed, "but it feels impossible sometimes. Like… who's going to care what I have to say?"

He listened, nodding thoughtfully. "I know that feeling," he said. "For years, I played to empty clubs. Crowds of ten, maybe fifteen people on a good night. I doubted myself constantly, wondering if it was all just a waste of time. But I kept going because… I had to. It was like I didn't have a choice."

Hearing him talk about those early years of struggle made me see him in a new light. I'd only ever known him as the superstar, the one who made success look so easy. But here he was, admitting that he had faced the same doubts, the same fears of not being enough.

We talked for the next half hour. He brought my attention to the idea of there being so much talent in the world. There were singers better than him, but it was about endurance, grit and belief. Just doing it would mean he had a leg up on those who were not doing it. He told me about the years he spent playing in obscurity, the endless nights on the road, the times he thought of quitting. I confessed my own fears, the voice in my head that kept telling me I couldn't make it as a writer.

Weaving his fingers into each other, as if he was sat at a boardroom, he leaned forward, fixing me with a steady gaze.

"If writing is in you, you can't ignore it. It's going to eat at you until you give it everything. It doesn't matter how long it takes or how hard it gets. The only way you'll ever know is if you do it."

His words struck deep within me, a truth I'd been avoiding. Here was someone who understood that ache, that restless need to create, and who had found a way through.

"So funny how coming to see your show is on my bucket list. Apparently, James, someone from my past, came to the concert and he said it was so electric he couldn't sleep for three days after." He grinned his delightful smile.

"Come. Be my guest. We are always on the road."

I gathered up my notebook, feeling a new kind of calm. I wasn't alone in this feeling at all. I had watched enough biographies about musicians that I should know, there is always a struggle.

"You've been very honest, and you are very inspiring Simon. It's been wonderful to meet you. Thank you."

"The pleasure is mine. You have possibly unlocked a little idea in my mind now. Seeing you, watching how you are figuring this out has taken me back to a time when I was in your shoes. Perhaps the next lyrics will fit there somewhere, you know, like, something about listening to the inner voice." He seemed thoughtful.

"I told my twins, if I had my life over again I would want to work in music. Too late now," I trailed off and we hugged goodbye. Jasmine would never believe this.

I navigated my way through the path back to our villa. As I arrived, I decided to take a breath and let the conversation with Simon sink in for a few minutes. I could tell her on the way to 7eleven.

Our clothes were unpacked and organised in a much more uniform fashion than I would usually do for an all inclusive break, sometimes I even flipped back the top of the suitcase and took the toiletries out and left the rest exactly where it was, but I felt differently about this trip. Perhaps because we had a lot booked, and would be busy. There wouldn't be time to search for clothes the following morning. As we knew we would be so back to back for the next two days, we decided to indulge ourselves with an early night, right after heading to the 7Eleven we had passed on the way in to the hotel.

12

Typically, Thailand

"Could this be any more Thai right now?" I asked Jasmine as we enjoyed the blast of the air con in 7eleven as she chose her toastie.

"This works out at 50p Mum," Jas said. The staff heated up Jasmine's toastie and I decided to stay cautious and bought just two macaroons and a Coke Zero. There was a mango sticky rice truck on the forecourt outside. I was excited to try such a thing. We heard so much about mango sticky rice. Ingredients that didn't go together, in my eyes. But the truck was closed, as it was too early I the day. I bought a mango smoothie instead. Sugar was everywhere in this island and I was concerned about athletes' foot. My body was never very good with too much sugar or carbs and the little candida bugs inside were opportunistic little sods and the second I gave them their favourite food or beverage of choice, they were off, causing infection. I needed to be careful. I had packed plenty of medications to try and keep my gut in order, and I had stuff for pain, ear infections, and vitamins for energy. But we needed that early night, so we loaded up on what we could and headed back to our villa just before the storm began.

Rain had not been forecast, but the wet stuff fell out of the clouds faster than I had ever seen before. Jas and I were settled in the best bed I had ever felt, and the noises from outside were calling me to film for YouTube. I narrated a running commentary and thought this was as heavy as the rain could get. I settled back in the bed and put my phone to one side. Noises of the rain got much louder, and crashes of thunder filled the air. The weather was epic. A smile covered my face wider than before, and my eyes opened widely.

"Oh Jas, this is incredible." I was filled with utter joy and I wanted to lap up this feeling of contented excitement. This place was my idea of paradise and as every minute ticked past, I received more affirmations of my initial impression. I slept soundly, until the next morning when we were being collected to explore the island, see the temples and those famous phallic rocks.

13

Golden

"We are on a trip today; can I possibly get some coffee?" I asked the woman who worked at the hotel. Our package was bed and breakfast.

"Oh? A trip?" She said and then gasped and looked concerned. I nodded, yes.

"Oh, please. Wait." She ran beside the communal swimming pool and I called after her,

"It's ok, honestly. Slow down." She carried on running. I was worried she would slip. Her face remained expressionless as if she was focused but also concerned at not providing us with adequate service. My mouth turned upwards, with my lips together. How endearing was this lady, this place, this island?

I love coffee, and I have fallen into a slight ritual which is potentially bordering on addiction or obsession. It isn't the caffeine I need, I protest. I love the idea of drinking a cup of coffee in the morning. When I am home, I boil the kettle, open the big black fridge door and put a small amount of milk in a mug. It fills less than one-quarter of the cup, as I know milk is not the best thing in the world to fill my gut with. It's made for cows. Cows are huge. I don't want to grow to the size of a cow. Of course, that method is something I have designed in my mind, and I don't know what the scientific papers say about it, but in my mind, I would try and save the ration of more milk for when I went to a coffee shop to write. Then, I swapped out recently for a flat white which served several purposes. It's stronger in taste. It has less milk. The barista makes pretty patterns in it which gives me a chance to compliment them on their art, which I am sure will be returned in Karma, and if it isn't, perhaps it will make their day. I read somewhere that if you look into the persons eyes as you give the compliment, it dives deeper than just saying it into the air. Sometimes I get shy, but I try the eye contact when I can. The baristas always seem to appreciate it, even if they brush it off like The Fonze. But at home, it's less milk, 3 in 1 Nescafe sachet, in the aim it will limit my coffee intake habit, and two squirts of sugar free vanilla. I pour a glass of water, add a mint leaf and I take those things to my office to record a little video of my beginning of my journal session. It holds me accountable, it excites me, and it makes me feel alive. There have been days when it has been difficult to find things to be excited about and so I will take this little ritual, if it puts a smile on my face. Could I have gone without my coffee before our day out? Absolutely I could have. But this was more a question asking if we could get something for breakfast within our two minutes before we got the coach. Jasmine and I would have arrived earlier for breakfast, but 8am was the earliest they offered it, and our coach was arriving at 8.15am.

The lady was so kind. She returned with a smile and handed us a carrier bag with plastic containers inside. She had lovingly prepared fresh fruit which had an array of colours. I didn't doubt it would be as fresh and juicy as the previous exotic fruits we enjoyed before. Two take away juice cups were filled with yellow juice and straws. Straight from the fridge, the pots were beginning to steam in the heat.

This was a holiday. I was determined for it to be. I watched her rushing about and I told her not to, but still she continued in haste. I was feeling patient and I was really proud of the person who I was in that moment. I felt nice. This felt like a slightly new feeling, although it was somewhat familiar. I dug deep to wonder what I was feeling about myself in response to this woman rushing about so much. I wasn't actually too sure but I knew that she was indicative of the person who I had been in the past. Somebody who was trying so hard to do so much and not really getting anywhere. Even though Jasmine and I really appreciated the boxes that she brought, full of delicious fresh fruit, the most juicy pineapple, a delicious dragon fruit slice, and some sweet melon, we had enough time to wait. And we were on holiday.

I wasn't used to holidays like this. Every other trip that I took had to be a business transaction. It was sad. But it was what my online audience seemed to want. Without me striving and being 10 out of 10 stressed I didn't know how I was going to provide for my family. I've had to be mum and dad since day one, but now I also had to be husband to my mum as well. It did feel like a lot of pressure and it was always obvious to me that there was no time for me to embrace the things that I wanted and the things that I needed. But maybe now life would start to carve out some time to embrace the writer. As a child, I used to sit down with big pieces of thin cardboard paper, which my dad brought home from the factory he worked in where he was making toilet rolls. I used to sit with various pens; sometimes it would be a chisel tip marker pen, other times it was a felt tip pen, sometimes just a biro. I would make lots of fancy lettering on this massive sheet. I would create signs for my mum to take to work detailing all the things that she was selling on her tea trolley. Happy to sit there for hours, creating brand new fonts that were created by the actions from my fair hands, I felt creative. The letters wore flicks and tails which you wouldn't usually see. It became apparent that this was my happy place. Alongside trying to teach myself to play on the keyboard, I was more than happy sitting in my room with some music playing in the background while I wrote anything to do with any sort of letters in the world. And here I was at 54 years old, still delaying the dream I had as a child.

Friends of mine were consistently telling me that my writing was good, and I needed to embrace it. I didn't really even mind how good it was or what kind of money it might make me to enable me to take care of my family, I just had to take the pen in my hand and do the physical act of writing. This holiday I had brought my journal and a small selection of pens. I wasn't sure if I was going to make a story of this trip or not. Nothing became apparent. I was just happy being in the now, embracing the sand and the palm trees and the coconuts and enjoying the people around us being so positive and so happy. This felt brand new.

Jasmine and I headed to the reception desk, where we were going to sit on the uncomfortable wooden sofas and wait for our lift. We'd only been there about five minutes when the minibus turned up to pick us up. It was a full-on party bus with speakers in the ceiling and faux leather seats with buttons and gold piping. We were the second people on the bus to go on the tour. Two gentlemen sat on the bus, speaking in an accent to each other. It was time to head to collect other people before we started to explore on what they called a half-island tour. Several stops would be made throughout the day, visiting the iconic places we had got to know during our research. We expected to see several Buddhas, of various colours from pink to gold, and some would smile; while some solemn. The day ahead was full of promise.

These iconic structures, had been filmed for YouTube on many occasions and famous and pretty much every video that we had to see. Despite the heat, I felt calm. I felt happy. I was enjoying being who I was.

In the local Thai language, 'Thank you' was a word I was learning easier than I usually did. it Some people may have attributed how relaxed I was that to the idea that I was on holiday. But I have had holidays which trigger me. I wasn't sure what I was feeling, and I was sure it would all become apparent, but I felt unrecognisable.

When the bus had a total of eight of us on it, the guide picked up a microphone.

"Oh, I guess I don't need that," he tossed it aside and laughed. He turned around to face all of us on the little minibus and kneeled on the passenger seat while the driver continued to wander down the road. "Good morning everyone. I can just call out to you. Welcome to this Samui tour. Today we have lots for you. Lots of nice. You will need to maybe dress in some appropriate respect at some." Jasmine and I knew what he meant, turned to each other, smiled and nodded. We had our clothes organised as a priority. Aside from not wanting to show disrespect, we also did not want to embarrass ourselves by arriving in the wrong clothes. We both had long, baggy trousers and I had a pashmina to cover my shoulders. That shawl carried a story. It had been travelling with me since 2008 when my new husband bought it for me in Venice, two days after we got married in a castle. I'd argued that the pashmina was too expensive, but here I was sixteen years later, almost as good as new and fit for many purposes. It served well as a wedding outfit accessory as well as a thin blanket on a frosty plane.

"First we head to Wat Plae Laem, which is a beautiful and active Buddhist temple complex here on Koh Samui. Known for its stunning architecture and vibrant colours, the temple features statues of the goddess Guanyin, the Buddha, and other deities surrounded by a large lake filled with fish. The peaceful atmosphere and intricate sculptures make it a unique cultural and spiritual site on the island," he explained. This was the lady with all the arms, whose name no one remembers. As we turned a corner in the minibus, I spotted the jolly Buddha. Sitting by the water, all pink and smiley, he was a true sight to drum home the notion that we were no longer watching a YouTube video, but we were looking at this chap in reality. We were on Samui; we had made it.

We stepped out of the air-conditioned bus and the heat was like opening the oven at Christmas lunchtime. Every time I felt that heat blast, I pursed my lips and said, "whoo," and looked at Jas with raised eyebrows. In front of us were some buildings with no labels, encrusted with gold. They glimmered in the sunshine. This had a feeling of Thailand. The edges of the rooves curled up toward the sky and the top of the buildings met at a point. The doorways were gold, the steps were striking and empty. Empty. Photo opportunity.

"You need the loo?" I asked Jasmine, as I pointed towards the toilets. The rest of our party pretty much ran to the iconic structures but even though I was determined this was a holiday, me and my daughter knew we must update our vlog. After using the restrooms, we stood with the golden buildings behind us, in the shot and started to let the viewers know we were at the first stop. I attempted to remember the name, but ended up saying, "I'll add the names on the screen and in the description box," as I pointed to the lady with the arms. She was encased in scaffolding, which felt like it was a pity. But I changed my focus in an instant and reminded myself that it really didn't matter. We were here, and that was a true blessing.

Spending time getting the right shots was important and both Jasmine and I fussed over getting our best look as we tried sitting on the steps. For some reason, maybe years, I could see what would be a flattering shot and instructed Jas to film me walking away from the steps slightly towards the camera, slightly towards the monuments. It worked. I didn't hate my look. I was happy enough. I was flattered that Jas copied the shot for her own film, and then we checked our watches. In previous times, I had learned to listen to the guide, and set an alarm on my phone for five minutes before we are due back to the bus; I was never late. There was only another 15 minutes left at this temple, which was fine, if we were quick. We had been asked to cover shoulders, but bare knees were ok here. My look was somewhat sophisticated for a woman in her 50s, and we were blessed to accidentally visit that part of the world in the off season. Locals said it was too hot, so people tended to come in the winter. That was great for us, because we almost managed a photo of just us and the statues, with the odd dot on the horizon of a suggested tourist. Diana and the Taj Mahal was in my mind, and while we didn't quite achieve that, I was happy with the beautiful views we had. Mostly I was facing the buddha and the Wat Plae Laem and I looked thoughtful and chic, but I wished my hair was slightly longer, or cut into a point, but it was short and that was that. Just before Christmas, I had 12 inches cut off to donate to a charity which makes wigs for little girls who have lost their hair. It was something I always wanted to do. My hair was long enough to touch the top of the cheeks of my bum. It grows fast. I knew I could grow it again, but a large part of me liked the shorter look, especially when it was curly.

"We will need to be quicker," I said fast. I checked the time on my phone again and knew we would run out of time if we didn't get this content quickly. The quiet of those steps became a distant memory too soon, but I did not want us to be the people who held up the bus, so we began to speed our way around the temples. My trousers were wet, I had perspired so much. Sweat dripped into my eye; it stung.

A small child of local origin, was feeding ducklings in the grass close by, and she was the picture of an idyllic child who belonged on a poster. We passed by without taking photos, and headed back to the minibus.

"Hello, hello. This one. Bus one." Our guide showed us a number on the front of our bus. There were two now. I wondered how many would show in the busy season here. That's the sad thing about tourism; the tourists. Spoils the view, and spoils the atmosphere. I often travel in the off season, and although this was unintentional, I was glad it was quieter.

As the bus pulled away, I looked back at the Jolly Buddha once again, wondering if I would ever see him again.

14

Views, Views

"Ok, we stop at Chawang, which is one of the most beautiful beaches on the island and we can take a stop for photo. Don't get the ice cream here, we have better ice cream at Hin Yai Hin Ta. Real coconut ice cream. Is the best there." Jasmine and I looked at each other and she took a deep breath and turned her head to the guide and opened her mouth.

"Is the ice cream dairy free?" She asked as she craned her neck.

"Yes. Coconut. Coconut milk ice cream." Jas was delighted. She could partake. I was a big believer in the health benefits of coconut, after my diagnosis of Crohn's. I started to add coconut oil to my scrambled egg in the morning. I was never a fan of eggs, and still can't label it as my favourite food. But I trained myself to eat them, just as much as I trained myself not to grimace at the coconut oil in my eggs in the morning. I am so sure it helped, among other things, as my symptoms dramatically reduced within three weeks. My gastroenterologist argued with me about the difference diet can make. Until five years later when I was still pretty well. He apologised and ate humble pie. Any excuse to add coconut to my plate was now a must. And I liked it.

We pulled into a small side kerb and hopped off the bus. I didn't feel too sure what this part of our trip was about, as it wasn't documented in the brief. I had to dig deep to trust the process without a frown.

"Now, maybe don't buy souvenirs here, you can do shopping later. We have fifteen minutes here for photo and toilet," he pointed to his right. I felt as if I wanted to use the loo, despite most of my intake of fluid coming out of my pores. I nodded sideways to Jasmine and we headed to the bathroom. En route, we were distracted by some very steep steps which ended at the beach below. I couldn't have climbed down or up, and I knew I would be satisfied by a photo. Jasmine took selfies, and I looked over the top of her head. In the distance, a very blue sea was shimmering in the gleam of the sun. Sprinkles of sunshine glittered on the top of each little wave and the sky reflected the depth of the blue of the sea. Chawang beach looked stunning. But a bit far down. We would visit there later in the week and perhaps stay for a day on the beach, I noted.

"Do you have tissue?" An English lady with an accent said. She could tell we were heading down to the toilets.

"Yeah, I'm sure," I started to rummage in my large backpack, convinced I had wipes with me. After too many seconds, the lady held out a half pack of tissues, which you would blow your nose with.

"You'll need these at all these types of toilets," she told me. She was well-versed in Thai toilets, unlike me. I felt slightly ashamed of the idea that I didn't know such things. People asked me about travel. People looked to me for advice, and here I was with no tissue for the public toilets. I was grateful for her and took the packet as I carried on toward the bathroom, which was a hollow carved out of a rock face. I looked inside. It was dark. There was a pungent smell of urine mixed with heat and probably sweat. On the floor by the toilet pan was a wooden bucket and a ladle to match. I stared at it long enough for Jasmine to catch up with me.

"Mum?"

"Erm, yeah,"

"Okay?"

"Might not need to go after all." Jas looked over my shoulder and her top lip turned up towards her nose. We packed the tissues in my bag and headed to the bus, knowing there would be another toilet somewhere soon. I carried on sweating anyway.

15

Big and Golden and Koh Pangnan

The stop which followed next was to the Big Buddha. I was sure more than one of the structures was named The Big Buddha in the world, but this was one we were familiar with, after our research. Standing at the top of the biggest staircase, we had been warned by YouTubers, and now from our guide, that it was going to be hot. The heat of the sun was increasing as the hours ticked by and I was thankful for the weather. I vowed never to complain about the weather after my experience in Greece, and even though I was finding it hot, I had trained for this. My health had been a focus since we booked the trip almost a year before. It had felt like a pipe dream back then, and here we were, looking at that familiar staircase from the shade of a beautiful bucksome bougainvillaea tree. Pink flowers were giving shade to us, as I waved a fan across my face and sipped my water.

"Ok everybody, take your time here. Enjoy it and see up there for the view of Koh Pangnan," he pointed to his left which was our right. I raised my eyebrows and grinned to Jasmine, I flicked my bottom lip inwards on my curled tongue in appreciation for being able to see Koh Pangnan. It wasn't that I particularly wanted to attend the full moon party, rather to appreciate the moon and the cycles it gives us. To see the island which hosted the party would almost feel close enough.

"It say take off your shoes," he grinned, "don't take off your shoes. Too hot. Too much burn."

I moved the straps on my backpack for no reason, and looked at the vision in front of me. It wasn't Everest base camp, but it was a challenge. There were steep stairs ahead of us to carry us up to Wat Phra Yai. The Buddha was 12m high and the statue was built to depict calm, purity and resolve. The left hand rests with the palm open and the right hand down over the knee. This temple was one of the monuments which carried tighter rules and knees needed to be covered here. Jas slipped on her baggy trousers over the top of her shorts and let the long shirt flow over the top of them. I knew we would want photos on the steps, with the Golden Buddha behind us. Ideal shot. We would sweat for the price of the photo and video footage, in the hope that it would be appreciated by those who watched. I looked down at the steps and focused on one at a time, lifting the long trouser legs as I went.

"Mum," Jas started to call and gave me instructions to take her photos and videos, as I was a few steps down from her. It was always my pleasure and I was so glad that it was still me who she chose for getting her content. There would be a day when someone else would be enduring the heat patiently because she wanted to get a better photo. Her beauty allured me, and she looked amazing at every angle, smiling or not, front or back, bin bag or gown. I wondered if I wished I looked like that. I used to. But the girl who I was when I looked like her wasn't as wise as Jasmines mum, and my wisdom has begun to show its beauty in my life.

Stepping down to my level, Jas looked at the camera and decided we needed some more.

"It's pretty hot Jas, can we be quick?" I wanted to head for some shade. Beads were running down my temples and melting into my neck. We moved faster, and she suggested we take photos of me, which we did, to remain in my archives as my arse looked like an elephant.

The top of the steps showed itself as the stunning beauty it was. There was a slight breeze. I smiled. The pink tree below held my gaze as I suddenly didn't run for the shade. I hadn't noticed a local man pass me with golden magnolias gripped in his palm. He had come to pray at the foot of this powerful temple. I felt intrusive as I watched him bowing and kissing the ground, then holding his hands in prayer to his face. I was fixated on his prayer, and I wanted to know more. I wanted to understand Buddhism. After a while, he left, and I took a moment to look up at the statue as it towered into the sky. There was not a chip, or a finger mark, or any blemish on this beautiful creation. We had to move to the shaded area, which created a square shape on three sides of the Buddha and the steps on the fourth side. At every few yards was an oversized cowbell hanging from the roof, with a large stick attached to it. Guessing it was to hit the bell with and make a gong sound, I smiled. I had set an intention to strike a gong on this trip as I searched around for things to add to my bucket list. In case I didn't see a big round gong, like they had on the front of the film credits, I wanted to strike one of those. They all had different notes, which was fascinating. Occasionally, the breeze would blow it against the wood, and there would be a sound made. Gentle notes escaped the gongs as we enjoyed the high views and the quiet breeze.

Jasmine took my phone from me and opened it with the password to take my photo and video. I straightened up my pashmina and corrected my windswept fringe. It was a pointless task, as it was wet.

After I struck the bell, I shrugged my shoulders in a childlike manner and grinned. Attaching the meaning of 'I've done it' to anything seemed to be a little bit of a theme with me. I needed to achieve things, even if it was going somewhere to ring a bell, high on a hill next to a big golden Buddha. I was happy. Hot, but so happy.

16

Mummified Monk

Our next stop was to a strict temple, to see the Mummified Monk.

The mummified monk in Koh Samui is known as Luang Pho Daeng, a revered Buddhist monk whose preserved body is displayed at Wat Khunaram, one of the island's most respected temples. Luang Pho Daeng passed away in 1973 while in a seated meditation position, which he maintained until his death. Following his wishes, his body was preserved and has since become a symbol of devotion and spiritual discipline for locals and visitors alike. Our guide introduced us to the local guide, who had an excellent English language knowledge.

"This monk, Luang Pho Daeng, meditated until his last breath. He chose this state, prepared himself for it, knowing he would inspire others long after he was gone. His body remains here as a reminder of discipline, but also of impermanence. He teaches us that life is a fleeting moment, and what we leave behind is not our body but our actions, our dedication."

Standing before the monk, I found myself struck by a sense of quiet awe. It was so quiet there. His face, frozen in a peaceful expression, seemed to radiate a calm that transcended time. I listened as a temple attendant explained the monk's story: Luang Pho Daeng had chosen his final moments as a symbol of spiritual discipline and the enduring power of purpose.

Hearing this, I began to wonder about the kind of legacy I wanted to leave behind. Writing had always felt like a calling, a whisper in the back of my mind that I couldn't ignore. But was I ready to dedicate myself to it with the same devotion this monk had shown, even if no one else ever saw my work? Could I pursue it for the love of the craft alone, regardless of recognition?

As I looked at the monk, I realized that his presence was more than a curiosity, it was a testament to a life lived with intention, to a purpose that reached beyond the constraints of his own body. His silent meditation seemed to ask me: Would my words, like his spiritual practice, have the power to echo beyond my lifetime? Could they carry forward something meaningful, even if only a handful of people read them?

His monk's tranquil form had an answer in its stillness. He hadn't known who would come to see him, or what impact he'd have on strangers. He'd simply followed his path, trusting that his dedication would resonate in ways he might never witness.

My clothes were stuck to my body and I didn't know if I would be able to take my shoes off and put them back on again. I could wait on the ground level and still see the Monk. Just a few steps separated us, but I was able to keep my shoes on at the lower level and respect this monk.

During our research, we had decided we didn't want to see the monk, in case it was a little creepy. It wasn't, I didn't think, I couldn't quite decide. I always love a story of something 'against the odds' and this lack of decomposing was likely because the monk had decided he would not decompose. The scientist in me took a moment to wonder if there was any truth in the story I had recently heard from one of my PhD students about the additives and preservatives in food allowing us to prevent decomposition for longer, but I preferred the story I was hearing in Koh Samui by far.

"Do you mind if I go?" Jas asked. I needed no words, as I handed her my phone for her to take the photos and videos I needed. I saw a gong, and I wandered silently near it, feeling as though this was not a gong to be banged. Instead, I took a moment to look at this monk, and show some appreciation for his beingness. In hermeneutic phenomenology, this would be called Dasein, which literally means 'to exsist' or 'to be here, to be there'.

He sat there, sunglasses on, probably as chilled out as he was when his heart was beating. What was the silent vibe I was experiencing in this locality? Inside a glass cube, he sat in his meditative position and just oozed sophistication. What the mind can believe, the eye can perceive.

Jasmine walked up the few steps with our guide, who was called Yaa. He informed us that if you say his name but in a low pitch, it means Grandmother, so you have to say it in a high pitch, taking an octave to the sky at the end of speaking his name, so that it is his name. He lowered his voice to Jas and began speaking about the monk. This was no folklore as we could see it, this was a real person in front of us. I meandered around beneath the platform and tried to look for some shade. I saw a cat, it made me jump. He stretched out in the shade. We both took our time underneath this temple. I didn't know how to thank the monk for his devotion to the unknown. But the feeling was very real inside me; he made a difference. I wanted to make a difference. I had always known that, but I hadn't managed to figure out exactly the way forward for doing it. Although I always suspected I was being guided to help other people through my words and writing. I looked at the roof of the building as I let out a quiet 'hmm' in my audible thinking state.

I left the shrine with a sense of clarity, feeling a shift within myself. I no longer needed the assurance of recognition to validate my desire to write. Like the monk, I could embrace my path, allowing the process to be its own reward. The legacy I wanted to leave would be written in small, quiet ways, in moments of honesty, in words I crafted with care, in stories that might carry meaning, even if only for a few to read.

Leaving the monk behind us, we drove to the rocks, which was only five minutes drive away. A woman stood next to a cute moped, which looked like something from an old film, based in Rome. She lit a cigarette and flicked her hair to one side. She looked as if she belonged on the island. Jasmine said she had seen the woman at one of our other stops, and we wondered if she was taking herself to the same places on the tour, but with the company of her cute moped. Was she a digital nomad? I was adding that name to my online stuff before it was barely a thing. But I never really made very much of it, and now I was too late. A saturated market full of young beauties was overtaking and my chances of making it big would only happen if I labelled my stuff up as solo travel or senior travel, neither of which were appropriate. To me, a senior would be 75+ and I considered myself young. Was I delusional or even wrong? I didn't think so. To me, age was an attitude rather than a number. I've known people of 30 who were older than me in attitude. I like it that way, and others seem to like it too. We never did find out the story of the lady, but I hoped to rub shoulders with more people like her in future, maybe in Bali or somewhere.

"We park here. Bus 1 and we come back thirty minutes. Don't forget the ice cream here and the shopping," our guide announced.

There were little shops, almost market stalls, almost buildings, at the sides of the walkway towards an entranceway which said over the top 'Hin Yai Hin Ta' and Jasmine prodded me and laughed, "Yin and Yang," she said; which is what I had insisted on calling the rocks because I forgot their names.

The light grey rocks were flat for a large part of the area. Some people wore headphones, listening to recorded voices on some devices, telling them about the folklore of the rocks. I was happy to just look, decide which parts looked like genitals, and soak up the fun of the atmosphere. What a crazy thing this was. I looked to my right, with the sea behind me. Sure enough, there was a penis-shaped rock facing downward. I was unsure what crack I should be labelling as the grandma section. There were many of those. Our guide wandered up to Jas and me and knew what we were doing. When people decide we are filming for YouTube, they crank up the attention to service just a little. Which is always okay, but we are usually already impressed anyway.

"This one," he pointed to the rocks I had just spotted, "Grandpa sleeping. That one," he pointed with his index finger out to sea, "Grandpa excited." There was a rock, a little stout, upright and proud. Of course, we sniggered slightly and took photos. If you didn't , that would be like going to London and not photographing Big Ben.

"Ice cream?" I asked Jas, and she replied with a nod up and down and a smile. "Would you like an ice cream?" I asked the guide. He answered quickly with, "ok, yes," and I didn't think he heard what I said. We, and our unusual blonde locks walked over to the places which sold coconut ice cream. I was excited to see actual coconuts for sale too. The outer edge of the case was removed on one side and it looked like it was etched with a burn saying 'Koh Samui' with a coconut tree emblem. Now, there was a bucket list item there. Drinking from a coconut had been on my list for a long time and the previous Christmas, I shared that dream over a late-night phone call with James.

"Let's do it then. Me and you, what do you say?" I smiled broadly and tried to disguise it in my voice as I replied to James' suggestion.

"Would love to, where are we going?"

"The Carribean."

"Yeah? Ok then." An air of 'that won't happen' was circling around my mind.

"Really, I mean, you know, the business is up for sale. When I sell it, I'll come and grab you with the tickets and we will go. We will fly sweetheart, we will do it."

"I'd love to stick that up as a profile pic!" My imagination was already on the island with James, drinking from coconuts and taking photos. I knew we would have the most fabulous time. I had to guess he never sold his business after we lost touch, but for sure he didn't arrive with tickets, flights and straws.

This was a time for coconut ice cream, and as our guide followed us, we used his knowledge and asked,

"Which is the best place?"

"Here. This one?" He said it as if it was a loose suggestion, and not a place where he had a pre-arranged agreement and possibly an affiliate commission attached to.

"Would you like an ice cream?" I asked him clearly, while I looked at his face.

"Yes, could do."

I gathered that was a firm yes and turned to the ice cream lady, "three ice creams please, one in a tub."

It was the most delicious ice cream I have ever tasted, and it was less than five pounds for three in a tourist hot spot. I don't know why I cared so much that we weren't ripped off, as I'm not usually overly cautious about money, but this made me happy. We left the guide chatting to the ice cream lady and Jasmine and I found a quiet corner of the beach, near the sand, which was covered with shade from the coconut trees. We later found out as we went back on the bus that Koh Samui was famous for its coconuts and coconuts are a good source of income for the island. I grinned as I remembered the logo of my online business, which included a tree I would have previously called a palm tree. I would never again call it a palm tree.

Finishing our ice creams, and successfully keeping all the insets away, we headed back to look at the wares in the local peoples shops. One of the shops sold jewellery, which I guessed Jasmine would love. She bought herself a hair clip which was so adorable. It had a mix of both chic and little girl. I always saw my children as my children, even though they were older now. People never think she is much more than 15 years old, and I don't like to correct them. Was I in denial at the atomic rate to which I was heading to death?

She took a while to decide if she liked the orange-y pink or the white flower clip, and I couldn't help, as they were both adorable. I'm not one for shopping, but I spotted some boho chic island girl jewellery made of shells. I was against the sustainability issue of using things like this for a start, and I always had it in my mind that I would get a star on a rope made of plastic instead, for this island jewellery. I used to play about with jewellery a lot when I was in my 30s, but now, I seldom wore any. My ear lobes were giving up on fighting gravity and going with it now, and so I rarely wore earrings. Chubby fingers seemed to only wear loose rings well, which was fine when I was taking a picture of my writing hands, or a Tik Tok video, but otherwise, the ring would be lost. And lost jewellery is never ideal.

"You can try," the stallholder told me as he held out the shell necklace.

I wasn't sure at all. But in the end, I bought it and I wore it that night when we went out for the night. My hair was beach wavy, blonde enough to look like a surfer and a slight sunny glow on my cheeks meant the shell necklace was well placed. I looked like an island girl.

Our final tour with Yaa was back to our hotel and he kneeled on the passenger seat once again and told us more about coconuts and dropped in a statement which changed the way I think, forever.

17

Safety

"We have no police here on the island. Well, they are there, if you need them. But you never do. We don't need them here. Very shafe."

I stayed silent. My head tipped to one side and I was sure I had stopped listening. I lost count of the amount of people who had told me how dangerous it is in Thailand. Have they been to Cairo?

The views outside of the window whizzed past as I continued to mull those thoughts over. Is it really that safe that you barely need any police? That seemed unfathomable to me, but it was a thought I loved. Piece by piece, things were affecting my energy and I had no idea just how much until later in the trip.

18

Bathing in the storm

The party bus stopped outside of the Zara Beach grand entrance. I was so proud, and hoped people inside the bus would look at how beautiful this place was. It was nothing like a hotel at all, and that is exactly what I hoped to find. This didn't feel like work here. Koh Samui was opening up a brand new me; one who I liked. Echoes of the announcement that police were not needed on the island stuck with me. Over and over I contemplated how amazing that must be to live somewhere where safety is so guaranteed that the police are barely seen. The warmth which ran through my body accompanied a smile as we walked back into the entrance of Zara Beach. Soon, it was time to get ready for the evening and go out for dinner. Before sun down, we had a few free afternoon hours to enjoy and we decided we would try and find a beach bar somewhere. Quite by accident we stumbled upon The Door.

Black sofa bean bags lined the beach on the entrance to The Door. There were Bali beds, and long tables with around ten chairs around them, shaded by the black canvas over the top. Unaware of this place, we just walked the beach, with our beach towels and now it was time to stop and take a breath. It had been a busy time since we arrived, and I was dreaming of sitting and thinking. Absorbing the atmosphere was often my favourite thing to do anywhere. I was never bored when I was thinking. My mind was busy, chatting, but I failed to understand how people could ever be bored.

"Are we ok to sit?" I pointed to one of the Bali beds. There were soft-looking rolled-up towels on the end of each bed, and I gathered this was one of those beach bars which you pay a little more for, but then you end up with everything you could dream of.

"Of course, of course," the man handed us wooden menus which looked like a menu you would find at a fashion show. This place enchanted me.

Before we sat, I noticed the place opened up in size, away from the beach. There was a swimming pool up there. It was small but good enough for a dip and maybe a few short lengths. It wasn't like the massive pools in the all inclusive resorts, but it was fixed to a wall of mirrors on one side, and pebbles surrounding the other three sides. The ladder into the pool had a wooden bucket and ladle at the side of it, to wash the sand off your feet, just like the Maldives.

I was sure we lost some consciousness here and there as we sat on the bed with our cold drinks. The people on the table next to us were laughing here and there and rousing us. They looked rich. They smoked something strong. They ordered big bottles of champagne, or something. I was offended by the smell, but I was intrigued by everything else. They lived here? Or were they visiting?

I didn't expect to see this vibe on the island at all. Something I would have missed about life at home is how diverse places could be. You could camp in a field, hoping the sun would burn away the dew on the freshly mown grass, or you could have caviar up the Shard. For me, the local Starbucks with aircon and friendly staff was my regular place to go and sit to write, or work, if those two things are different. I liked that about home. But this feeling was at The Door, too.

Dipping in the pool was fresh. The water was warm everywhere you went, except the shower in our room. I floated about for a little while and left Jasmine to rest on the beds. There was a man. He was on his own. He looked thoughtful as he looked out at sea. He was about my age. He was handsome.

I had planned to head to the end of the pool closest to the sea, but that's where the man was. After giving things a second thought, I did swim up to there. I wondered if he would speak. I wasn't going to. I wasn't sure I was looking my best, but I did float around there, leaning on my forearms which were propped on the side of the pool, and I wondered why I still noticed men. I shouldn't really. Not really. I had enjoyed two of the wedding's of my dreams, I had been massively and deeply in love several times, and I had recovered from devastating heartbreak. I didn't need a man in my life. I had all that I needed, I thought. So why would I notice him?

19

Coconuts

People were ordering coconuts from the menu. They were labelled as 'young fresh coconuts' which is why they were so green. Inside of the green was a harder shell and it seemed they cut the top off and placed a straw inside so you could drink the coconut water. A spoon was served so you could scoop out the flesh. 'The Door' was burnt onto the side and I had hoped to enjoy one which said Koh Samui, so I waited for that experience until another day. There was still some rosy glow needed for my cheeks, and my beach waves looked a little more as if they needed some teasing yet. So I decided to give it a couple more days until I experienced my first coconut, and subsequent solo photo shoot.

After what seemed like pure bliss, Jasmine and I dipped into the sea and soaked up the essence of the ocean for quite some time. We had no idea how long we were there for. Above those famous light grey rocks was a dark grey cloud. It was moving in our direction and we decided we should probably begin to pack up. Everyone else started to think the same. We were in for a huge storm which would likely cut all the electricity, and give us a dramatic light and sound show.

I looked at Jasmine and gave her a nod and she nodded back. Slowly we started to walk towards the shoreline out of the ocean and it was a shame to have to leave that lovely warm water. We thought it would be a good idea to organise our things and walk back to the villa before the rain began.

After we paid our bill at The Door, knowing we would be back soon, we started to walk very slowly towards the villa. Our shower had been cold the day before and we reported it to reception. Hoping it had been fixed, we knew that we needed to shower off the remnants of the beach which you always carry back with you. A cocktail of suncream mixed with salty sea and stuck sand needed to be showered off in the room. As Jasmine managed to shower in the cold water the day before, I thought it was only right that she had the first shower. We settled into the room and put the air-conditioning on. Just as I was organising our bags from the beach, Jasmine called out, "it's warm!" I was overjoyed. I looked out the window over the dipping pool to the clouds above. It was difficult to see exactly what colour the sky was because we was totally in the jungle full of trees, but between those trees, I could see a glimmer of darkness starting to appear almost as if it was becoming nighttime. It didn't get dark until about 6 o'clock in the evening so I knew it wasn't time for that yet. I heard a rumble in the sky, and the expected storm began. There was something about extreme weather that I seemed to find exciting, so long as it was safe. I knew this was a safe storm for some reason, and I listened to the rain as it began trip by drip off of the roof above me. It played a melody alongsided the sound of the shower which Jasmine was in, enjoying her wash. There was a crash, and a flash of lightning but I couldn't see where lightning came from. Underneath my breath I said a very quiet "wow," to myself. After what seemed like around 15 minutes, Jasmine emerged from the shower with the white towel wrapped around her little white body. She had little blushes of red on the shoulders and on the end of her nose. Her hair was wrapped in another towel.

"That was lovely," she said. I was about to pick up my towel when there was another flash of lightning. The lights inside the villa went off. We heard a click, and assumed that it was the trip switch going. I picked up my phone and switched on the flashlight. I knew the electricity fuse box was just inside the wardrobe. I opened the wardrobe carefully and shone the flashlight inside to illuminate the darkness. I wasn't sure what the click was because all of the knobs were switched on and nothing tripped at all.

"I don't know what that was! It's still switched on." Jasmine shrugged her shoulders at me and we tried the light switch again as if for some reason it would magically switch the electricity back on.

"I hope that doesn't control the hot water." I laughed and I took my clothes off to get into the shower. I reached out my hand to the silver handle and pulled it towards me to start the water. Nothing happened. There was no water. I tried it once more as another bolt of lightning flashed through the twilight apartment villa. There was no water.

"There's no water Jas." I heard a muffle of her response to

me. My clothes were off already and I wrapped the towel back around me, unsure what I should do. The electricity could be out for several hours and I definitely needed to wash the sand off of me.

A playful twinkle shone in my eye as the next rumble of thunder ripped through above us. The rain was a tiny trickle outside and part of me thought that about standing outside and be showered by the rain, but it wasn't heavy enough. Before I did any more thinking at all, I walked outside with just a towel around me. Unwrapping the soft white towel, I placed it on the seat next to the dipping swimming pool outside. There were leaves floating in the water, and the pool would be as warm as a bath and once I was inside the water, nobody could see me naked. My naked body began to step into the tinged green water.

I thought of him.

I grinned slightly and my eyes softened. I took another step into the water. The warmth surrounded my salty skin. I sat down on the edge of the pool to ensure I found the bottom of the swimming pool with my feet. As soon as I could feel it on the bottom of my feet, I slid under the water up to my shoulders. Within four seconds, I was in the pool. My body felt alive. Joy began to pump through my body. I reached my hands down underneath the water onto my tummy. I held myself there for a little while with both hands. There was a certain feeling that began to emerge at this moment.

I lifted up my tummy to wash underneath with my other hand. Since I've had the twins, since I've had the Caesarean, that part of my body always needed extra care taken of it, and salty sand would only make it sore. I lovingly took care of this part of my body regardless of its lack of beauty.

Initially, I had the notion to just be in the pool and wash myself while the shower was out of action, but this dip turned into so much more than that. I stopped for a moment, and just embraced the present. I lifted up my chin and looked at the trees above me and listened to the noises surrounding me. I took a deep breath and exhaled while smiling. The air was fresh. There was warbling from the animals that were surrounding me in this rainforest. The trees were rustling with the slight breeze. The warmth surrounded the top of my head and my salty curls. I took a mental picture to try and embrace remembering this moment forever. This was true paradise, and I wasn't sure I had ever felt so contented. I felt a feeling in my nose which always made me feel as if I was about to cry. I realised that there was absolutely no point, in allowing those tears. I grounded myself and placed both of my hands around my belly button as I held my body underneath the water in a loving fashion. He would've been so proud of this moment. He would probably told me that I'm a good girl, as if it was adventurous. He would have thought it was a liberating moment. I agreed. This was a liberating moment. Being naked in the middle of the jungle outside of a beautiful villa in a wonderful island full of friendly faces and people smiling and laughing with a lack of outward stress was just the absolute epitome of perfection in my eyes. And my imperfections in my body were always present. I felt my energy. Part of me wanted to tell him what I had done, and how I was feeling right at this present moment in time, but to message him would just be the wrong timing. We had to stay silent from each other at this time. I had tried to distract myself with James, but that didn't help at all.

In my mind I knew I was embracing this moment. And in my mind I knew that he would, love my openness of embracing my body in this way, releasing inhibitions and feeling so free in a way that I've never felt free in my life other than when I was in his arms. I slightly smiled at thought of being in his arms, he always made me feel safe. he would sleep while I refused to close my eyes. I would look at my hand laying on his chest and watch him breathing. I took in the colour of his skin and the smoothness of his body, and I knew the feeling I had then was exactly everything that I ever dreamed I could feel in the presence of a man. He gave me that. He gave me that, and it could never be taken away.

Occasionally I would dare to lift my eyelids to look at his face. He would breathe through his mouth when he was sleeping. It was safe then, he wouldn't see my obsession. I looked at his long, dark eye lashes and his handsome face. His skin showed no age. His collapse under my embrace gave clues of a life less-lived. I never asked, he never mentioned, but there were powerful unspoken words. I would drink in the memory for the fear of it being the last chance to store away the perfection of the moment. He would wake and top up my need to feel his security before it was time to part again. He would pat the top of my buttock, where it met the small of my back, which I knew was code for, 'it's time.'

I craved him.

I had craved him for all of my life. Even before we met, twenty years before, I missed him. When he was with me, womanly energy flowed with ease. At least I had felt that.

I had felt total devotion to a man who filled my heart with so much love and passion. I knew what we had was immeasurable, and even though time had passed, I still felt the same and I still stayed by this notion. Involving myself with somebody else was pointless. No one would ever measure up to how I felt when I was with him. I would allow myself a few moments to capture and remember the feeling of my palm on top of his chest as he moved in rhythm with his lungs. Looking at him, feeling him, tasting his lingering kisses in my mouth would bring the moment to life. When he wore his aftershave, I would smell him on me all day. Sometimes I would follow up our time with a simple text.
'I smell of you.'

Knowing he would read that while he was at work gave me reason to smile.

A part of me had always expected it to end. I was a powerful manifester. I hadn't expected it to end the way it did. It was almost two years since I had seen him. Those feelings never lingered before. Was that because of him? Perhaps it was my choice. He wasn't as perfect as I allowed myself to believe. He was infuriating at times. He was opinionated, and he could be cold. He repeated himself at times, which was unnecessary as my memory was as strong as an elephant when it came to him. I remembered everything, including him not liking to take paracetamol. I clung to that statement as if it was an attack on me while I was trying to keep my pain at bay. It wasn't, of course. It was him showing me how strong he is; he knew I liked that. I also liked the feeling of his vulnerability which I felt as an energy when he would kiss me for the first time in a week. A little inaudible sigh would escape and I could feel him relax into my body. We all want love, don't we?

Maybe there would be a day when I would tell him what I had just done in the pool, but maybe not. He helped me to feel confident within myself and so liberated that I was free enough to throw my towel to one side and get into the swimming pool with no clothes on. Even though he always argued it was something I had done myself, it wasn't. Feeling love from a man like him, having a reason to smile and to begin believing in my own merits was a new belief. Other people can help you feel that, of course. I argue the notion that you have to do it yourself. That inner programming has to be hard wired by yourself but the beliefs can come from external sources, in the same way abuse or negativity can.

Being naked in the pool may not seem like the most dramatic moment, to me it was a scene where I totally embraced my freedom, my confidence, and my love for myself, which was so often a void in my life. I always felt I was a fantastic human being, (but the words of others and the hurt that had been caused) had prevented me from feeling that in its entirety. I wished people would see me in the same way I saw myself. For some reason in this swimming pool none of that mattered. I was there, I was alone, I was just completely being myself and being totally in love with myself in a way that I don't think I'd ever felt before. I wanted to stay there and soak up this feeling. I was unsure of how safe I was in the water if lightning was going to strike. Even though the trees above me were keeping me safe, and I felt completely safe on the island, I knew I would have to draw this moment to close and get on with the rest of the evening as if I hadn't just totally had a moment with myself to potentially top all the other moments I'd experienced with myself.

It was time to get out the water and wrap the towel around me once again, I looked over my right shoulder to check that there was nobody walking nearby the villa, and all I could hear was the sounds of the animals. I stepped out in my nudity and put the towel around me, tucking it underneath my armpits.

20

Coco Tams

There had been a slight debate about where we go for the evenings.
I've looked up somewhere called the Elephant Club, and it looked
outstanding. I thought it was a kind of bar which you could sit in day
all night, and the vibe changed depending on the time of day.
Jasmine had found someone called Coco Tams which she said was
the place that was 'all over' Instagram. Not only did I want to make
my daughter happy, but it may complete sense to go somewhere
where we could create some brilliant content that people were
looking for on Instagram. Even though I was still determined to call
this holiday, getting the right content was important. I had no idea
what my future was to hold, but I really hoped that I could see some
growth on my YouTube. As the Elephant Club and Coco Tams were
both about half an hour taxi driver away, we decided to go to Coco
Tams. We had had a quick look online and saw the amazing fire
shows that happened at night time there. Although by the time we
made the decision and got ready for the evening, it was completely
pouring with rain. It was falling from the sky, creating a rhythm on
the roof and splashing into the pool, so heavy that we spent some

time filming from behind the safety of the window because we'd never quite seen anything like it in England. It dramatically dripped off of the leaves that were cascading over the roof. We decided to carry our rain macs, and carefully planned how to keep our cameras dry inside our bags. The Grab was going to cost us about £8 to go to Coco Tams by taxi, and within minutes the driver arrived in a very clean car. By the time we arrived in the town of BoPhut, he pointed to us where we needed to go which was near some coconut trees. He couldn't quite drive right up to the front of the building because there was a no through road there. The car we travelled in was clean and modern, I liked that. The seatbelt worked too. Unlike the ones in Tunisia, which I'd experience recently when the driver told me not to do it up with one simple word: 'kaput'. The rain had slowed to barely nothing by the time we arrived, and we walked through the street, avoiding the huge puddles which were reflecting the lights and creating soft ripples with the base of the music we could hear in Fishermen's village. We hadn't realised that Coco Tams was actually in Fishermen's Village, right next to the night market. We began to walk alongside the front of Coco Tams to find the entranceway. There was a staircase with words written in every down step of the stairs to spell out "Bad Decisions make good stories – You can't do epic shit with basic people."
I turned to Jasmine and grinned, "this is brilliant Jas."

I felt as though I was seeing little signs everywhere to guide me towards being writer and embracing the person that I was. I agreed, this is something that I really should've been doing. It was just a case of putting the wheels in motion and getting things done. I'd never felt so clear. I felt warm.

We were greeted by the staff in Coco Tams who said we needed a booking really but they could fit us in.

"Is there a fire show? "Jasmine asked. The hostess shook her head and looked woeful. "Well, I don't think so because of the rain, but we have to see what happens." We completely understood, we were not the tourists who were going to complain about such things. They couldn't control the rain.

"A different day maybe."

Although we hadn't realised it was so far in the taxi. We didn't mind spending the small amount of money to get there. There was no room for us, yet they put us on a very long rustic wooden table that seated eight people. They said we would have to share it with other people. Jasmine looked concerned and asked if another table had become available, could we move to that one?

After the usual conversations about gluten free options, and a quick move to a table in the middle of the restaurant, we had ordered our meal; which ended up as possibly one of the best meals I have ever had. I had pork, which was pan-fried and accompanied with rice, followed by my first ever mango sticky rice. I was excited to see it delivered to me in a coconut shell bowl. Another click of my camera before eating.

Life felt completely wonderful, and I was overwhelmed with the dreamy day we had. We paid our most expensive bill on this trip, which was still only equal to £48, and decided to visit the night market before it closed. The DJ had just finished his set in Coco Tams, and we were thankful for the amazing music, atmosphere and food. How could life feel any better than that?

21

Leaving the night market

Interesting sights engulfed us as we walked through the narrow walkways and I was fathoming the children being awake at such a time of night. A good thing, I suspected. A believer in life lessons being learned in the classroom *and* in the world, I felt inclined to endorse parents who home-schooled their children to see the world. Imagine as a child having so much fun with your cool parents, on the road, soaking up all that the globe has to offer. School felt unhelpful and unhappy for me, and while it was a place where I wasn't under threat from the sharpness of home, I never felt at peace.

The children in the night market were running around while their parents packed the stalls away. Faux designer bags and sunglasses were organised back into boxes, while kids played with bits of plastic which had broken off from the clips holding things together. They laughed and almost tripped on the passing tourists. Above their heads, other stalls with smelly food housed circular plastic bags, wafting flies away. A mechanism was attached to a four pronged coathanger-type of gadget as the bags dangled and twisted around and around. Flies still took their chances, but tended to lose more often than they won.

Coloured lights changed as we walked between the stalls. We reached a cute place which was not ready to pack away. The buzz of the food area was alive with music and people drinking beer. Green baize on the floor created an area where it was acceptable to place tables and chairs to listen to the late night sounds of the local band. There was an energetic hum.

Leaving the end of the road felt like a good thing, but I wasn't sure why. The area was busy and slightly chaotic. Was my energy being sensitive? Inside, I felt a similar feeling to one of fear. I wasn't unsafe, I knew that. There were darker shadows beginning to appear as the market packed up for the night. We needed a taxi and we couldn't find the road.

"They dropped us off and we had to walk a little to get to Coco Tams, remember?" Jasmine said. She was right. We were shown the right direction to walk and we headed that way before seeing the lines of coconut trees, high up above us.

We needed to find a road before we began walking. We were not on a road, rather a pedestrian area. We opened up our Grab app and started to look for a place to go where we could call the taxi. The road was full of holes and risen slabs which were threatening to trip me up. Since my diagnosis, I adopted a new fear of falling. Stairs were the worst. So I always held on to the rail. I didn't want to appear like an old lady. To me, the image of my little AS card in my purse was imprinted on my mind. It was alerting people to take care of my spine and neck if I were to fall as there was a higher risk of fractures. Knowing how to research, I had seen the incidence of the risk was only higher if your bones had started to fuse. My bones hadn't started to fuse. And if I could keep healthy, and not fuse, I would. I aimed for my health to be my focus 100% of the time. But people got in the way of that, time and again. Anger was my natural reaction but I fought to stop my emotion from showing. Looking after everyone else was something I found joyful, but I would never be in a position to look after them if I let these autoimmunities get a grip on me. My health and me, all the way, in the most unselfish manner possible. If I had learned anything from Mum's illness, it's that you must try your absolute best. Laying on the sofa, and expecting everyone else to do everything for you is unrealistic and impractical. You have to try. The weight for someone else to carry is too great. You have to try.

"Ohh, wait Jas," I said as I tiptoed over a hole in the pavement, "I'm going to need a wee soon."

"Are you?"

"Yeah, well think about it, we have another half hour drive once we found the cab." We decided we would try and find somewhere to buy a drink, use the toilet and call a cab.

Passing lines of shops with 'Massage' written on the windows, we noticed the ladies smiling at us. They had long lashes and long fingernails. They were stunning. I flashed a half smile back, thinking how I didn't fancy a massage at all, and carried on walking. In the distance a booming sound of some bass echoed. As we walked we noticed there was music approaching. That sounded hopeful. The band playing was a welcome sound which got closer as we walked. My body craved to sit, have a pee and drink some water. I needed to take a minute.

A big glass window framed the image of the band, with a lady sitting on a stool with a tambourine, tapping as she sung. This looked like a pub. We walked straight in.

"Hello ladies," the singer said on the microphone. I raised a hand in a half wave and shyly looked over. The room was full of local people but the Fishermen's Village area was typically for tourists. I hadn't realised we were travelling out of season. People came here in the winter months rather than spring or summer. This was the off season, hence the rain and the intense heat. I didn't mind at all. I usually travelled in the off season in Europe. It was cheaper, and I liked the UK during summertime, except for those stifling three or four days a year where we all decide we need air conditioning fitted in time for the next summer. Travelling out of season to Spain or Turkey for three nights was part of my job. It was confusing for people to figure out what my job was.

"Any more holidays booked?" I would be asked the same question frequently. But it wasn't a holiday, not really. There would be time to dip my toes in the sand, and perhaps have a paddle. If I was smart with my time I could sit on a sunbed in the shade with my laptop and do some editing. But my idea of a holiday was to sit quietly by a campfire somewhere in the middle of a field and just think. Going to hotels to look at the nutritional content of the foods had fulfilled my job as a nutritionist and that had branched into so many avenues. My first proper job was at a holiday park, then hotels, while I trained at college as a chef and then hotel and events management. I would answer questions for people in my Facebook groups who asked how warm the pool is in September, and I had kind of accidentally become a travel vlogger and travel writer. I did love that job, of course. But my purpose on this earth wasn't that. It wasn't providing a service for people who wanted to book a holiday. They ask me the questions, get their answers, then go book it elsewhere. If they booked it using my affiliate link, I would then get paid. It wasn't working. People in the UK were the ones able to use my link and they were so suspicious of clicking an affiliate link unless it was one of the huge sites, who wouldn't realise was an affiliate company. But it helped to pay some bills and I loved it. I also ate really healthily and moved a lot while I was at the hotels. I was an expert on what made a good hotel and what didn't, and it had been my job since I left school and went straight to catering college. I wasn't the worlds greatest chef, but I was a great manager and my career soared fast. I was blessed. But recently, things had got tricky and I was delighted to take the job offered to me teaching nutrition at the local university. I loved that job. And it helped me to feel smart.

None of these things were the life purpose. I knew what my purpose was, and I had known that since I was little. The feeling of calm and peace came when I was writing. That didn't mean I was the worlds most impressive writer, or I could change the world. But

I believed I could change a few lives. I wanted to inspire other people and I felt I had been dealt a tricky hand to enable me to do that.

Travelling out of season was something I was used to. I was also used to people staring, just as they were doing in the pub in Fishermans Village because we weren't local. Usually they stared because I was solo. I wasn't uncomfortable in the pub, but my back was hurting and the stool at the bar seemed to beckon me to sit.

We ordered our glasses of water, I used the toilet, and thankfully, Jasmine managed to get a cab to come close to the pub in a few minutes. I couldn't wait to get back to Zara beach and sink into that soft bedding. I never did get to the bottom of my uncomfortable feeling through those streets.

22

Elephants

8:45am was the pick up time for us to go to the elephant sanctuary. Jasmine and I had spent a lot of time researching what makes an ethical sanctuary. We wanted to know if these magical animals are rescued from cruelty or not. We were confident we had chosen the right place. After another hurried breakfast and a take away pot of sweet fruit, we hopped into another party bus to go to the elephant sanctuary.

Eat Pray Love had a scene in the film where Julia Roberts' character, Liz, was sitting by a tree. It looked as though she was journalling when an elephant appeared. She froze in fear, then stumbled as she stood up and backed away. The elephant began walking towards her and after a short spell of time she realised this animal was not there to cause any harm. They exchanged quite a moment before she ended up holding the top of his trunk and giggling. I wanted that moment for myself. I had instructed Jasmine to take a photo of me hugging his trunk.

Driving up a dirt track road, through some clearing in the jungle, I smiled. My eyes softened as I drank in the view ahead. I was certain I could never take such a view for granted, even if I saw it every single day for the rest of my life. The sights were so different than anything I had ever seen before. Something about this level of nature felt polar opposite to the feeling in the night market the day before. I was sure it wasn't related to safety, or having a vibe, but it was my energy. Was I beginning to listen within?

Jungle trees looked vibrant, green and lush in this rainy country. As the truck bumped back and fore, we climbed further into the natural jungle. Long grass laid scattered among the dense trees in the distance, holding themselves tall and still in the heat of the day.

"Ahh," came in chorus from our fellow passengers and I gathered they had seen something cute. Despite cranking my head like an owl, I missed whatever they could see. A click of the handbrake suggested we had arrived. The handle at the back of the bus was opened and local staff called out, "welcome, welcome."

"Oh we are here."

Strict vibes were coming at us in the form of instructions for what to do and where to go and we followed like soldiers across a natural-looking enclosure. The fences were made of rough-sawn wood which was latched into each other unevenly. Sinks were lined up by a shady area, surrounded by varnished wood. A lady stood close by the basins smiling and nodding to us as we all stared and walked past the area. I guessed we would be using the sinks at some point, but we continued to walk past until we reached a tent which looked rather like a stretch circus tent. Under the shade were rows of polished dark wooden benches and tables. I slid myself all the way to the safety of the end and Jas took her seat next to me as we waited for everyone to filter in.

After a few minutes, we were given a gentle safety briefing. I sat on my hands while the guide was calling his out words as clear as he could, to ensure we all understood.

"The elephants might get jealous about the food. Don't tease them as they might be angry. They can't see you if you are behind them so don't stand there." He didn't mention the strength of their trunks, which I experienced when we fed them for the first time. Filming everything, another staff member had watched me make the little balls of nutrition for the elephants back at those basins we had walked past earlier. Jas opted for me to make it all up. I was instructed to use banana and make it into a pulp to mix the nutritional powder into. We were assured there were nutritional supplements inside and the nutritionist within me was glad to see these animals being treated so well. I used the left over banana skin to cover the little balls. The yellow toppings were a garnish, another piece of food, and a photo opportunity. I looked to the camera and assured the viewers I knew exactly who I was in this moment.

"I have cooked for thousands of people over the years, but never have I made food for an elephant," I smiled at myself. It was important to me to convey a sense of who I was, and part of that person was a nutritionist who had previously been successful in catering for the rich and famous at huge sporting and social events. The Grand National was one of the most prestigious events I was lucky enough to work at, and the FA Cup final in 1999 was the one that got away, as my legs were in stirrups while I had my IVF embryo transfer. Manchester United beat Newcastle 2-0 and I would have met some of the greatest footballers of the time, including David Beckham.

Life was less chaotic, but felt more concerning. I was never sure if that was due to having more time to worry or if it was true reality.

Trying to convey my importance to the people who watched my videos, I was creating the identity I hoped for. It seemed to be an excuse and a justification to tell them I was there in the capacity of researching, filming, and doing all the things except the one thing which I felt was my purpose. I hoped it gave off the impression of my intelligence. It was exhausting spending a lifetime trying to convince others I was an ok human being.

"Come across now with the plates to here," the guide pointed to a direction which was beyond the rough sawn fences. We had a clearing of dry, dusty ground to stand on. Within a few seconds, the group of people began to gasp. Several noises alerted me to knowing there was something to look at soon. Then I saw them.

Grey elephants began walking towards us as if they had no concept of time. Swinging their trunks from side to side, they majestically meandered down the hill towards our clearing.

"Hup. Hup," the elephant handlers kept charge of the animals as they walked towards us. Fences kept us away from them to a level, although the enormity of the powerful animals meant they were very able to break through the wood if they had a desire to. We didn't know much about their story, except they were rescued from being used for people to ride on them, or some other cruel act. Now they lived here, free to roam, eating their nutritious little balls of food with banana skin garnish, without a need to worry anymore. Jasmine and I insisted on researching the ethical sanctuaries. We knew it was important to only support those who treated the animals the right way. But I knew my Eat Pray Love moment was approaching.

It was no accident when the staff member put one of the elephants in front of me. She had terracotta marks on her ears and trunk, with little grey/brown dots scattered in contrast. I felt connected to her. I looked her in the eye. Time stopped ticking. There she was.

What was her back story? Who had hurt her? How was she now? Did she bear the scars of the past? I wondered if she was still hurting, still doubting herself, still feeling a sense of not being good enough while she innocently went about her day. I looked her in the eye. I questioned if the moment was as majestical as I had been told. Would she never forget? Would she always remember me? Would she wonder what my back story was? Would my food be the best she had ever tasted?

We were rushed into offering the elephants some food. I looked into her eyes one more time and she waved her ears back and forth. I stepped forward to give her some food. The little ball sat in the palm of my flat hand as I stretched out my arm. A long muscle swept through and swiped the ball from my hand. I stumbled backwards and caught my step on a blunt rock which was cemented to the floor by the natural ground. The strength of the trunk surprised me. Why wasn't I ready to experience the force of this giant beauty? My legs began to feel the effects of the adrenaline within my body and I took a deep breath in. My lungs did have air in them, but it seemed to be escaping me too quickly, in rhythm with my palpitations. Bang, Bang, my heart thudded. I wasn't sure I wanted to feel the elephant anymore.

"Here, Jas, you go," I held out the plate for her to feed this mighty animal. The trunk waved around between people who were scattered like a scene from Cats, as we were overshadowed by the elephants. Our elephant took a ball from a woman at the side of us who had outstretched her arm. She was refusing to give the elephant the food and instead, she threw it, as if it would catch it in its trunk. I didn't think the elephant could see the food at the end of its trunk. The food fell to the floor and remained in its little ball shape. The trunk looked like a little hand as the end of it hardened to feel for the food on the floor. She knew it was there. The man who was with the elephant reached down to pick it up and held it near the end of her trunk. She coiled the end of her trunk around the food and scooped it towards her little triangle mouth before swallowing it whole. She had me mesmerised but it was hard to ignore the thumping in my chest. Why was I feeling overwhelmed? Confident I would love these animals, my inner self was confused. I gathered I was becoming more afraid of things going wrong as I got older, which should be the opposite. Possibly, after looking at old videos of me, I had realised that just as the spark inside me had started to dim, I had to accept the realisation of the life I had lived, and the hurts I had endured. It made for more unnecessary anxiety.

Stepping back, I took out my camera to film my stunning daughter, who was lit up by the intrigue of the elephants. She was loving life with them and didn't seem at all worried. Occasionally, she needed some reassurance, and while I wasn't going to be asking for reassurance, I was having to pay attention to the way I was beginning to feel. I was uneasy. I wasn't the only one. The woman next to us was feeling the same way. She and I didn't want to be too close to them. They were powerful animals; majestic. I took my time, as much as it was possible in this hurried environment, and looked at the elephant again. Her markings were artistic and she seemed to be welcoming. I wanted to stop feeling so concerned at the strength. They seemed clumsy. How could you walk with those trotters? How didn't you trip on the trunk? How could they see a size 4 human foot close to their own foot?

We took turns to feed the animals. I was comfortable behind the camera, despite telling myself there was nothing to fear. An announcement alerted us to the bathing area for the elephants. It was time for them to be hosed down for some reason and we were assured this would be something magical to see.

Back at the stretch tent, people were stood high up, behind a fence. I spotted an opportunity to film the elephants from there, roaming freely and being hosed down. There was a baby elephant called Junior, who loved to be close to an adopted mother called Maria. He seemed less clumsy, but he played the fool among them. He trumpeted, to the delight of the crowd, and me. I was smiling as I witnessed elephants do in fact, 'trumpety-trump, trump trump trump.' My camera was capturing the memories for me to recall at any time in the future. This trip was going to plan perfectly, and the travel vibe was strong. I usually felt something totally different within travel, as I was going to hotels and sharing facts, without too much of an emphasis on a vibe. Yet, this day felt like I was truly seeing the world. There was a magical air, despite my anxieties and I was open to soaking more of this feeling.

'Phhhrrrr' echoed through the sound of the running water from the hose and the guide called out, "Junior farting," and laughed at the end. There was a ripple of sound from the crowd and the guide repeated, "farting." I had that on film, which was going to be incredible for my YouTube channel. I was excited to share all of this, to grow my channel further, and to know I would be able to see the world while filming everything and writing my books. I wanted everyone to live their best lives, despite the challenges. And a farting elephant was more than a delight, especially as he trumps through his trunk too.

Junior was rolling around in the mud, close to Marias feet as she was drinking from the orange hose the guide was holding out for her. He seemed like a character from a comedy. There was an air of Disney about him. I wanted the moment to last. I sat on the decking beneath me which was warm to the touch. My legs seemed to have less blood running through them as I was crouching. The heat always seemed to want some of my energy. I crossed my legs and held my camera in position. Without looking through the lens, I watched these two elephants having fun. Their bond was clear to see as Maria tilted her head towards Junior and lightly brushed him with the underside of her trunk. She loved him. Just as I loved my twins.

Next, we were instructed to head back towards the lines of basins for our refreshments. Plastic cups were passed around as fruit juice cartons were placed o the tables for us to help ourselves. Despite sitting under the thatched rooves, the heat was inducing so much sweat. My cheeks were red and swollen. The battery operated fan was a true blessing for me as I held it close to my nose. I knew we would experience fabulous heat in Asia but it was hard to imagine the feeling of being so hot until you were there surrounded by the energy of the sun. Living in the UK, it was still early May and there was dew on the grass in the mornings, and early evenings commanded some sort of winter coat.

"Ok everyone. Everyone. We ready?" We nodded as we were handed some hessian bags with the name of the elephant sanctuary on them. Wondering what they were for, I looked inside. There was a bottle of water in there. Traditional pointed hats were given out to us to protect our heads and we were guided through a gate and up a slight incline on a hardened dirt track road.

"Must all keep together here," the guide said as he walked faster than I would have liked. Jasmine was walking next to the man and he was speaking to her. I wished I could hear better, so I could eavesdrop. Doubtless she would be finding out all about the elephants and the stories about how they came to be a part of the sanctuary. Would I get to know that information or would I continue to lag behind next to the old woman next to me?

My dancing legs pushed hard as we reached the top of the incline and the sidings gave way to some lush green trees which nestled into thick jungle. The hard ground was dusty beneath my feet and I was glad I had worn trainers, although I was beginning to regret the decision to wear shorts. Somewhere I had overheard there were king cobras in this part of the world. Was that a fact? Was it a joke? Why wasn't I more clued up? I had prepared for this trip like it was an all-inclusive resort in Alicante. Being used to all inclusive, things seemed simple. Perhaps I should have done more than watch a few YouTube videos to prepare for this trip. A few days before we considered packing, I had seen a gorgeous couple who I follow online had come up against something dreadful. They advised that they had contracted Dengue fever. I knew it was bad, as there were photos of them on hospital beds, wired up to two drips each. I started to read their post. I learned you can get bitten by a mosquito who would carry Dengue and have this awful disease put you straight into a hospital bed. The couple reminded us that you can get bitten day or night. That was a new piece of information for me. I had only ever used repellent in the evenings. Jas and I had stocked up on the special pink fluid we had read about online which we bought from 7eleven and we wore it day and night. And kept our fingers crossed.

Was I prepared for long grass and potential snakes?

How did I feel about standing next to an elephant's foot?

My anxious brain continued to be in charge.

Jasmine walked at speed next to the guide and swung her arms with force. Our moods contrasted each other as I tried to keep up. Sweat dripped onto the ends of my fringe and slowly streamed into my eyes. The salt stung and I closed one of my eyelids in a squint.

Ahead, the fast walkers seemed to be slowing down and they began to look out to their left. My pace flowed as I meandered towards them. As I got closer, I noticed a clearing in the pathway and lush green blankets of grass were encased by the tallest coconut trees I had seen. The jungle was breathtaking. Then I spotted my elephant.

She stood silently, picking up grass, bamboo and bananas from the floor.

"They eat 500lbs of food each day. They pretty much eat all day."

My feet stopped where they were, just shy of the rest of the group and I stared at the elephant, eating with a backdrop which resembled a work of art. My teeth unclenched and hung heavily as my lips parted slightly. This was the most incredible sight I didn't even imagine. The elephants wandered in the jungle. Freedom was surely a reward for them after a life of cruelty.

Taking turns to stand next to the elephants and have photos taken, I knew this would be the perfect moment for the photo I had dreamed of.

I couldn't.

I just didn't want to touch the elephant.

There was something about its enormity which gave me a sense of powerlessness. Standing four feet away, I remembered the highway code rule about driving past bicycles. Assuming they could fall over, you needed to leave enough room so you wouldn't drive over their head with a thud, thud. How far did I need to stand back from the elephant?

"Come," the guide waved me forward.

"I'm ok here," I said. He laughed in response. I was struggling to be close to the elephants. Considering their own feelings, I wanted to respect them too. Thoughts of the weight of the elephant foot next to mine ran like a train in my mind next to the idea of snakes living in this grass, the sun beaming on my damaged skin, the shorts I was wearing, the salt in my eyes, round and round.

"Let's see the other elephants now, we will go here," the guide pointed ahead to the far side of the jungle clearing. My eyes followed the length of the coconut trees toward the sky. I would never tire of such a stunning view. Could I stay on Samui forever?

We began to walk toward the elephants and the sun started to prickle my legs. I wasn't sure if this was fictional, born from my insane creative mind. I stopped and stood still as if my boots were made of concrete.

"Hello!" I called, "Hello, excuse me. Hello!" I called in quick succession. "I can't. I can't." There was no capacity for regret or remorse. My feet would not move. I was standing, waiting for permission to move from the guide. The heat of the sun touched the top of the pointed hat and I wiped the top of my lip with my index finger.

"OK??" the lady asked as she unstuck her lip from her braces.

"I'm sorry but I want to go back. Is that ok? Can I go? Is it safe?"

"Oh, wait, you want to go back?" She echoed my question.

"Yes, I don't want to go over there." Jasmine saw I had stopped and she needed no explanation.

"You ok if I go on Mum? I want to go on." I nodded to her. She had a voice, she was assertive, yet still a sweetheart and I was so glad she was who she was. My angel. Be safe my love.

"Let me get someone to take you," the lady guide said as she waved her hand to tell me to stay there.

"Thank God for that, can't bloody stay out here in this bloody heat," a voice said from behind me. Ignoring the voice, I remained glued to the grass.

"Come," a boy called from the pathway. I turned towards him with a sense of relief, aiming to move fast and omit the anxiety of getting back to base camp. The jungle life was not for me. I felt clear about my emotions, and I was annoyed at myself. Caring about missing out was taken over by my mind once again. Could it please piss off just once? In front of me were half a dozen majestic elephants smiling at me, with their waving ears and gentle nature, the tallest trees I had ever seen, and I was concerned about things which were unlikely to happen. Anxiety could be a bastard.

Mumbling seemed to follow me. Between the still of the beating sun and the sound of my feet crunching underneath, I could detect an Australian accent. Someone else seemed to want to walk back too; someone I didn't have the capacity for.

"Bloody heat. Too bloody hot for this." She raised her voice towards the guide and shouted, "Too bloody hot. You shouldn't send us out here like this, in this heat. This is bloody ridiculous. It's too bloody hot. I'm likely to pass out in this. I do that. I pass out. You know, I pass out! Bloody ridiculous."

As I reached the young guide, I asked if it's ok to walk back. I had no definite answer as his broken English ended up as a nod and a smile as he stood still. Next to him, I felt safer. I was sure of my decision to head back. He seemed to be looking behind me, back into the jungle. Quarter turn by quarter turn, I faced the same direction to see an older lady walking towards me. Her feet were moving as if she was stepping over sinking sand. The grass was long but that was not needed. *Just walk. Just move. Let's get back.* The guide smiled as she continued to mutter and shout alternately.

"Bloody ludicrous. There should be ICE PACKS. Ice packs you need," she used her hands to mime putting something on the back of her neck. I wasn't sure an ice pack was a good idea or not. She straightened out her hair which had frizzed in the heat and wiped her sunglasses. "I pass out you know. I do that." I didn't even half smile. I wanted to get back.

She reached the guide and I and the sun began to prickle my legs again.

"I pass out you know. Especially in this heat. Bloody ridiculous that they sent us out without any ice packs." She bellowed to me and looked at the guide. "Should have ice packs." He nodded up and down up and down with a smile. He had no idea what she was telling him and he continued to smile as he held his hand in front of him to demonstrate where we would be walking.

Back down the pathway, we got out of the clearing until we were surrounded by the trees close by once again. The air felt the same. The woman continued to repeat herself.

"You need to walk very slowly in this heat," she commanded. Driven by anxiety and fitness, I was proud of being able to walk fast and keep myself healthy. Dance ensured I would not be the one to pass out and I wondered if perhaps she should try a little jive once in a while. It makes you happy, it feels good, keeps you fit and gives you incredible friends. My health was improved for my fascination with dance which had followed me for most of my life. Wanting to walk fast, I took my pace down a little for her benefit, until more instructions followed,

"You need to walk slowly and in the shade, find shade wherever you can and walk in it. You can't walk that fast in this heat, you can't."

The voice in my head answered her, 'I can.'

"Bloody ridiculous sending us into a jungle with no ice packs," she carried on, "Women of our age can't be doing that."

My gaze stayed on the floor. Women of our age? Our age? Without a doubt, she could have been my mother. I decided not to be offended. Either way, why does it make a difference if we are women and how old we are? Fitness is the key thing here, and lack of anxiety.

"Could be bloody snakes out there."

I nodded while my eyes traced the floor in front of my feet.

"I sometimes just pass out. I do that," she continued complaining while we walked the path. Subconsciously I walked past the gateway we should have ventured in to. Her words were rumbling away and I ignored her as best as I could.

"hello, hellooo," a voice called after us, "this way please, this way. You can't go down there." I hadn't seen our guide leave us and I had just continued to put one foot in front of the other and decided to leave my voice alone and focus on breathing; something my neighbour could have felt great benefit from, and potentially prevented herself from passing out. She needed to use her oxygen more wisely.

Turning around as she called after us, I realised I had walked too far. Imagine a random elephant stepping out in front of you. I apologised to the guide.

"So sorry, I didn't realise I had gone too far." I smiled and brushed the fringe out of my eyes. "Can I take this off?" I began to remove the hat which felt as though it created more heat in my body. She nodded back at me and held out a sideways hand and slid it through the air in a straight line, which looked as if she was presenting me with a quiz show winning prize. I followed the direction of her fingers. Another staff member was stood in the shade with a tray in front of her. It was stacked with melting ice packs for our hot necks.

"Thank you so much. Oh Wow, thank you. Lovely," I smiled, "that's lovely, thank you."

"About bloody time. Sending us out there with no ice packs," she shook her head in fury, "can't be sending people out there without ice packs in this heat."

Her complaints were irritating. I could be patient with most people, in the best of times and the worst of times. Now, I was finding a sense of calm was illusive. After a period of anxiety, I could be exhausted. I needed solitude and peace. The trees promised to deliver that in the comfort of the shade at those shiny wooden benches. Wanting to sit there and drink some water, I craved for her to shut up.

Looking back at the hero holding the cold tissue ice packs, I smiled again to prove we were not all behaving so shockingly. We were not the only people in the heat. So far, we were given the very best of days. They had done their best.

The stool beneath me gave me a chance to take a breath as I sat in the shade. I exhaled. I felt a presence pulling up behind me coupled with, "Hi, I'm Johanna. That's with an H." Turning around against my will, I laid my gaze on the table and said, "I'm Lou."

"Did you say, Lou?"

"Yes, like Louise, but please call me Lou. I feel as if I'm

being told off if I'm called Louise." It was the fastest way to explain my name. I had needed to re-educate people in recent years. New friends see my profile with 'Louise', but no one sees Mum, who calls me Lou, the kids call me Mum, and there are no older friends in the same circles anymore. Bit by bit, Lou was becoming unknown and Louise was replacing it. I lost a sense of self, as I had never been Louise, except for Grandma, who was always displeased with everyone. All the people in my life who called me Lou were dead or incognito. Changing my profile name to Lou did work, but it was such a tricky name to introduce yourself as. My standard introduction was laid out to Johanna, and that should have been quite enough conversation. I began to turn back to face my bottle of water.

"Could be snakes out there you know."

Realising I was being rude, I responded, "I was a little worried about that, I would have no idea what to do if I saw a snake."

"Oh, English?" she sneered, "yeah, I bet. Well," she proceeded to educate me in the world of snake spotting. The life history followed. "And now that I'm 74," I wondered if this was the moment for me to say, 'You're not!' but I kept silent. My mind thought back to the moment in the jungle when she remarked about women of our age. She had given me twenty extra years, and brought me much closer to death. I was angry but I was beginning to see a picture of a lady who was likely insecure and damaged. Who would behave as if the world owed her a favour like this if there wasn't enormous trauma attached?

"Well after here I will be going to Bali for a bit. I was here with my husband who had to go on to do some work, a bit early. He told me to stay and enjoy the rest of the trip. I offered to go home with him but then he needed to also go to London and so I'm staying," she continued to fill in many blanks of the story in great detail. I was hearing a different story as she told her version. She wore a wedding ring, but that meant nothing these days. I wore mine when I was in certain countries on my own. Not Samui; not Thailand. I had never felt so safe. Who was she convincing?

Johanna continued to complain to the staff without thinking about them. The staff continued to smile and run around serving us while they were also hoping to prepare our lunch. I could smell a fryer close by. I watched, expressionless, as she spoke to the staff like my Grandmother would have spoken to me. 'Louise' would have been less gracious in response than the staff were. Louise would have looked at the ground, shoulders hunched, without verbalising or reacting. Louise would not have been rescued by her mother or brother, and I wondered if I should try and say something to Johanna about the vermin she was producing. The staff continued to run, bow, smile, fetch things and be more attentive than one could expect from another human. "Of course," they would bow, "Yes, no problem," would accompany a softer smile. I was smiling inside at the experience I had of seeing such kindness in the world. Furious at the experience they were having at the mercy of Johanna, but I was feeling as if I began to experience a sense of home. I had always carried a deep hope of people being nice and loving to each other. As a child, I felt the void of sweetness. As an adult, I projected too much sweetness onto others, which frequently attracted a broken heart in one way or another. Being 'too much' was a curse. All I hoped for was a world in which we could love each other in all the appropriate ways we should love each other. So far, I have not found such a thing. Poles apart, Johanna and the local staff showed me exactly what I was afraid of, and what I was hoping for in clarity so obvious, I could not ignore what I was feeling. In my 54 years on the planet, I had felt lost because I was different. Like an avalanche, I downloaded a feeling which propelled me into a tsunami-type wave of realisation. What if I wasn't the strange one for being a sweetheart? At work, I was introduced affectionately as the poppet. Perhaps this was a good thing. Maybe the love I had inside me didn't make me misshapen, but rather this could be a strength. Did the ugliness of Johanna just launch me into a new belief that I should step into the 'Lou-ness' of being me? There was something about watching her which gave me unspoken permission to be who I wanted to be. I had put it on the back burner of life for so long, for fear of being ridiculed. I hadn't had the perception to realise I was being irritated and programmed by the lack of affection and encouragement as a little girl. An electrifying moment hovered around my aura as I sat silently. I held my mouth with a cupped hand as the blur of Johanna's words rumbled in the background. My brain was comprehending something, which was taking a moment to fathom.

What was I feeling?

What was I thinking?

Who had taken over my brain?

Realising there was a story to be written about this journey, an excitement buzzed inside my belly. She had woken me up by showing me I'm not a bad person. I did deserve all there is to be offered in life. I must not hold back any longer; I must step into my truth of being a writer. After all this time of writing every little thing, it was time to take this dream seriously.

23

Oneness

Oneness is a conversation we hear many times in the world of spirituality, but I found it hard to accept. How can there be connectedness with such nastiness? I wanted people to be kinder, sweeter and just have time to love each other better. I would always be there for people who needed someone to talk to, a shoulder or a tissue. Accepting Johanna the way she was didn't come naturally to me, but I was trying. Nice people, like the locals, were easy to love.

Listening to the vile words coming out of Johanna's mouth was giving me some clarity which felt like a lightning strike. Her body language solidified her words and I realised in that moment, I couldn't consider speaking to people in such a manner.

Growing up, I was given many reasons to believe I wasn't such a great human. I believed it. Words echoed, as if they were in a feature film. 'Look at her pushing those tears out, squeezing them out. She will make a good actress,' was just one of the lines which glued into my memory. Would it have been so hard to hug a crying little girl? A small child tries to navigate life and some find that easier than others. As a girl, I found life confusing. I didn't know why until much later in life. Goodness knows what I will have learned by the time I am 74, but Johanna should know better.

Inner child healing comes in many forms. Some months before, I was sitting on the wide windowsill in my bedroom. My feet propped up against the side of my bed to take the strain off my back. He was lying on top of my blankets, on the other side of the bed. He tapped the mattress next to him to suggest I lay with him. He pulled his right arm up into the air, showing me there was a place for me to lay within his armpit. But I needed to focus, so I shook my head.

"I need to concentrate, and I'll tell you this from over here," I said, knowing that being close to him I would lose my thoughts. I had rehearsed this speech three times in my car the day before. I had even recorded it *and* listened back to check it made some sort of sense. It didn't make sense to me either. But if he and I were to make a future, he needed to understand me. After the twenty-minute speech, I still hadn't cried.

He stood up. "You can either decide to keep pulling that heavy thing along with you for all of your life, or you can decide to let it go and feel lighter and freer as you move forwards," he mimicked dragging something along with his hand. I walked around the bed and he enveloped me with his arms, holding me close to his chest and I breathed deeply. As I let the air go, a certain wave of indifference flowed. It had felt like a relief. In the calm of his embrace, I felt his complete support on a deep, emotional level. He held me tighter and just let me settle there for a moment. We stayed close until he needed to leave for work. The rest of the day was written off. Exhaustion crept through my body and I sat on the sofa for the majority of the day. I set my coffee cup on the windowsill next to me and I felt a presence in front of me. My third eye pictured a little girl, in a white gown. She stood with hunched shoulders and a dipped chin. Her hair needed brushing. She was sad. My eyes filled with tears and for the next two hours, although I was not crying, not sobbing, the biggest and wettest tears rolled down my cheeks as I continued to feel sadness from the girl beside me. There was no fear in me, but I sensed confusion and decided to meditate. I played some music on my iPhone and closed my eyes. More tears dropped as I mediated. Breathing deeply, I could still see the girl from behind my eyes. She had a green number seven on her gown. This reminded me of a photo I had seen of myself one Christmas as a young girl. I stood in the living room of the house where we lived, and played with some plastic fruit I had been given as a gift. The 'presence' was me. The inner child had arrived. She was hurt and emotional; she was empty. She needed something which was not going to be provided for by her parents. I wondered as I emerged from my meditation if I would be able to give her what she needed. I wanted to give her love, and fun, and make her laugh. Remembering the times I drove my school age children to get their education each day, I gave myself credit. We would play music to get them in a tip-top vibe for the day. Occasionally we would dance in the safest way in the car while we drove. They would sing along and dance and leave the car happy, even if the school day knocked it out of them. I wanted that. I wanted someone to make me feel good about going to school. Instead, I pretended I had a dog sometimes. It was a collie, like Lassie. Or there were times when my legs felt like they were walking in treacle, and that was the day when my friend, who was a giant, would pick me up and place me on the school grounds. My imagination was the thing which helped me with my sadness.

The day after our big talk I decided it was up to me to give little me what she needed, as if she was a different entity to me. I could be her best friend, her mother, her confidant. I would play and laugh and imagine putting her In the car seat next to me and give her music to dance to in her chair. It was time to see if I would be able to heal that inner child. I was forever thankful for being able to have that conversation about my lack of love and the constant hurt. He gave me a safe space to be able to lay those wounds out; that was special.

24

Waking up

Johanna continued to whine. I continued to try and cope with what I was feeling. Although it didn't make sense to me, there was a new realisation. As Johanna was so awful, and I recognised that, it meant I was not as terrible as her. And if that was the case, there were worse people in the world than me. So, what I had been taught as a child was wrong. I slouched on the stool and tried not to breathe in the smell of the fryer. Everything was suddenly new.

Being a decent human could mean being deserving of good things after all. Knowing about energy and attracting what you think about was a blessing and a curse. I had held off from magnetising good things to me as I was always a person who didn't deserve the best of things; I thought.

I sat for about three minutes and could only hear a far mumble from Johanna as my own thoughts took over from the complaining I was hearing. Seeing someone like her, like Mum, nasty people with sharp tongues, highlighted to me just how lovely I could be. Our friends at dance would ask to have a cuddle or cry on my shoulder. My place was not under the bright spotlight, inspiring them all with my world class dancing. I danced for fun. And they danced to escape. And when they couldn't escape, they ran to me and my broad shoulders. I had always recognised these things and gave myself credit for helping them feel better. But did that automatically qualify me to live the life of my dreams? Or would I continue to look for ways to criticise myself, just as I had been taught?

Over the years, I had wasted time and energy while trying to heal myself but in that moment it only took one sharp-tongued lady to make me wake up. Deserving the best in life was designed for people like me too. I began to run over muddy questions around the topic of me living the life I always felt I should live. Creating books to inspire people and help heal the world of the problems it had. Raising vibrations of people so they can help with the energy soaking into the earth would be my life's work, my purpose. Johanna had made me realise that even I deserved good things. I deserved to embrace the loving side of myself, and to reward myself with taking a leap of faith into publishing more, getting more bestsellers out there. Heck, possibly I could live a life of my dreams, if it was successful. Could I be booking the house at Zara Beach again? I would stay for a month or two and sit on the veranda and write more books, with the sound of warbling in the background. My idea of the perfect life.

Johanna showed me how loving I was. She was no less deserving than me, but she gave me an extra belief that I shouldn't hold back anymore because I was a terrible person. I wasn't bad, I was great. I had a lot to offer the world and I had stopped shining my light because I was embarrassed. Someone like me? Who would listen? But now, I knew it was all wrong.

My water glass was getting warmer, but I sipped away to replace the sweat. In the distance, near the gateway, were our people. They were returning. I was pleased to be given some relief from Johanna, who told her story to more victims, and I was excited to see my daughter.

Jasmine skipped back to me, red and sweaty and she beamed with a wide grin. She looked happy.

"Oh Mum, they were fabulous!" She had enjoyed her adventure into the jungle space with the roaming elephants. No sooner had she sat down, when food began to stream out of a little hut where the fryers were filling the air with smoke. My food was a gluten free dish. A strange fried egg was served up to me. It wasn't a fried egg like you would get in English breakfast, but rather it was a whipped up omelette but deep fried. I struggled to eat it. If I had made something like that at home I would have had to add cheese on to it; lots of cheese.

After we ate our meal, the staff brought red watermelon out on platters. Chopped into tiny triangles, we lapped up the juicy fruit and made ourselves sticky, all the way down our arms. I wasn't sure I had felt clean on this trip at all, but although there was an option to get into a bath with the elephants next, I was still fearful. The guides explained the necessary steps to ensure this type of bathing was still ethical, although we discovered much later that any bathing is discouraged as it's not really a natural habitat event. We felt devastated that we had supported somewhere other people would suggest was unethical. Our opinion remained as we witnessed the elephants being treated with love and care, so far as we could witness.

Strict measures were put into place telling us to shower off our suncream and to ensure hands were washed to prevent contamination for the huge grey friends. Waiting on the sidelines to film, I had washed my hands and took a seat on a bench beside the little pool.

25

Resorts

There is something about returning to your hotel after a trip. All your things are there, you get to know the staff and you can easily grab whatever you need.

After a refresh, we headed to the beach for some swimming in the sea. I gathered you would never tire of the warmth of the sea, judging by the number of locals who pulled up on a moped and walked over the soft sand to get into the sea. This was my idea of paradise and I instructed Jas to bring the waterproof case so we could take photos in the sea. It was almost time for me to get my coconut photo too. The shot was waiting until I had more curly hair, and a slight dash of suntan. I knew I would look stunning. I was wrong. My face looked red and swollen, so I left the coconut picture until the next day.

Our final day in Koh Samui was thick with black clouds blanketing the sun in the sky. It was cosy. It rained on and off and I could think of nothing I would rather do than eat my coconut inside our favourite beach club, The Door.

Settling on the sofa, the breeze from the electric fans kept us cooler as we flicked through the menu.

'Young Coconut' was listed. Even though I had wanted one with Koh Samui burnt into the side of it, I accepted it saying 'The Door' and ordered one. A break in the rain allowed us to wander outside and get that shot. It was important. A bucket list item was going to be ticked, on my paradise isle. The photo would be my new Facebook profile picture and the person who was supposed to share that coconut drinking moment with me would realise my strength as I went ahead and drank the coconut, with or without him. He said he would be there. Over and over, "I'll be there."

I sat on a fallen trunk of a tree and Jas pointed the camera at me. My hair was a mess. I needed fake tan. My cheeks were so large, my eyes looked closed. I wouldn't be adding the photo to any profile picture at all. He would be the one missing out and it was only important to one person to tick off that list; that person was me. And I had done it. I waited for him for too many years. Still, I wanted him to know I would carry on with or without him.

26

Take Two

Leaving Samui was sad and good at the same time. I had decided it was the finest place in all the world, and I wanted to stay for a very long time. But it was time to head to the excitement of Bangkok and to see our friends. And we had heard good things about Koh Samui departures airport.

Bean bags lay scattered on the grass, under the swings. Everything was free there; tea and coffee, juices and snacks. If somewhere was designed to make me happy, it was Samui. Knowing I would be back, I embraced the energy around heading to the next place, which was China Town, in Bangkok.

North v South, these two places were poles apart and it was hard to imagine they were the same country. They were the same. Kayaks were replaced by beeping Grab taxis, and lapping waves were gone to make a place for street markets lining the back roads. An air of dust and light smog hung in the air above the traffic.

Our bags were firmly in our hands, and we attempted to check in to the hotel, being too early. They stored our things for us while we sat and waited to find some of our friends. A group chat had suggested we would all be heading somewhere for some food or a coffee.

The strangest feeling is always bumping into someone you know on the other side of the world. Even though we knew they were all coming, we recognised them one by one and seemed shocked every time. As always, we hugged each other. Some of those hugs were long and deeply felt. Others were just a quick hello. Occasionally, there would be no hug exchanged, but more often than not, this was where we went for our quota of love.

More friends arrived and we all had our luggage stored and decided to leave the hotel to find some food. One of our friends had thoroughly researched, knowing many of us had dietary needs. He was someone who worked high up in a food company, a bit like I did before I had the twins. We bonded over conversations about food and driving the same car, and he confessed a few sins. Either I had the same 'naughty' twinkle in my eye too, or again, it was due to my broad shoulders.

27

Thipsami

Pad Thai was a dish I was sure I wouldn't be able to eat. But my foodie friend said he had researched a lot, and I could eat it. I still didn't know what it was, but I saw photos of it which contained noodles. Usually, noodles are made from wheat flour, and that would be a disaster. My phone had answers I needed and I pulled out the all knowing piece of tech and searched Thipsami Pad Thai:

Pad Thai is one of Thailand's most famous and beloved dishes, a stir-fried noodle dish that blends sweet, sour, salty, and umami flavours. It typically features rice noodles stir-fried with eggs, tofu or shrimp, bean sprouts, and garlic chives, all coated in a tamarind-based sauce. The dish is usually garnished with crushed peanuts, lime wedges, and sometimes chili flakes, allowing diners to adjust the flavour to their taste. Pad Thai's balance of flavours, its light texture, and the fresh crunch from the bean sprouts make it a globally recognized favourite.

When it comes to *Pad Thai in Bangkok*, one place stands out: *Thipsamai*. Located in the heart of the city, Thipsamai is often regarded as the best and most iconic spot for Pad Thai.

Thipsamai is a historic restaurant in Bangkok that has been serving its famous Pad Thai since 1966. It is located on **Maha Chai Road**, near the Giant Swing, in Bangkok's Old Town. The restaurant is often packed with both locals and tourists eager to try its famous dish, with queues forming outside its doors every evening.

In summary, Thipsamai offers a quintessential Pad Thai experience in Bangkok, blending history, flavour, and authenticity. It's a must-visit spot for anyone wanting to taste one of Thailand's national dishes in its most revered form.

I was sold.

We never did find the swing. But we had walked very far in the heat and dusty air, I would go and sit there anyway, even just for a bottle of Coke Zero. But he was right, it was gluten-free. And I was overjoyed.

Walking into the restaurant, my mood was irritated. The chaos and the heat, and being hungry and a little tired, with no space for my own time, was taking its toll on me. Determined not to become a Johanna, I tried hard to smile. Inside the restaurant, it was easy to feel happy. This place was hard work but a traditional feast for the eyes. The small tables were too tiny, really, and the seat was a short stool, which I felt sure my butt would not fit on. Chopsticks were laid on the tables, and I was excited to try eating with them.

Double checking with the staff was met with disdain. They seemed aggravated that we had asked about menus with dietary requirements. They were busy. I understood. But this was important. I needed to walk back to the hotel, and without knowing if I was avoiding gluten, there could be a crisis ahead.

We couldn't fit on one table, so we split into two and still managed to take a photo to show our other friends back home, who didn't manage to make it. My taste buds were in awe of the incredible flavours in this food and I suddenly fell in love with my version of safe Thai food. I liked pad thai. Doing things my way was going perfectly and I was feeling happy.

The time ticked past and we missed the first hour of check in, which didn't matter at all. But heading back into the arty, eclectic hotel was a treat indeed. Me and my camera would have so much fun here. We were soon in the room, looking at the purple walls and filming before we messed the place up with our unpacking. It was time for us to settle into Bangkok.

Dinner was not planned for the night so a few people filtered in to the group chat to discuss us going somewhere for our food. I was excited to be out with all our friends and I bonded nicely with another 50+ dancer who agreed to be my partner in our category. I had a sense of being blessed. Navigating the streets was tricky as it was so hot and busy. But we wandered like elephants, in a line until we reached a café bar. Signs were displayed, alerting us to the idea that no drinks were to be consumed on this day due to a religious holiday. No silly party/drinking games for one day at least. I was terrible at drinking.

"Selfie time everyone," the designated photographer called

out. We craned our necks and smiled. The photo was added to the group chat instantly and I smiled as I downloaded a copy for my son and text it back home to him.

"Are you ok? You two aren't sitting together?" I hadn't even questioned why until that point.

28

Empty nesting

To live a simple and happy, yet full life is something I have strived for year after year. There always seemed to be something to worry about. I wasn't sure if my own emotional hunger, born from a lack of hugs played a part in the idea of being addicted to sadness. Questioning if I would be better without sadness in my life, I enjoyed the minutes of laughter and music which filled my ears with a joy, taking away the tinnitus for a while. Just as things seem happy, a splash flinches' at me as the bubble loses its sphere. It can be indescribably confusing.

Children couldn't possibly realise the heartbreak which accompanies them growing up. Devoting a lifetime to this point, for a successful outcome means standing back and watching them stretch their wings to fly, one feather at a time, without a glance backwards to check the parent is ok.

Let me say, the parent is not ok. She is lost and alone and can't help but wonder where she finds joy between now and death.

She will work it out, she always does, but she must suffer in silence in the process for fear of asking for attention against their will. She never begged their father; it was better he walked away than stay under protest. She made *that* work with them in her belly and no money, job or home. This would certainly be easy in comparison.

He hurt her on purpose. They just hurt her because it was rime to soar. She knew she was thankful but the pain could't hear gratitude.

She clung on to every minute with them. Each simple affectionate glance would be soaked up like a sponge.

My emotional hunger was because Dad was too afraid to show love. That's as simple as it is. But if you are starving, you binge, you feel sick. It's not helpful.

"Don't worry, I'll be ok. I'm used to it, everyone does it to me sooner or later." I expressionlessly winced at myself. That was probably nasty. But it might have been true. I expected everyone to leave and stop caring about me and I would try with all of my inner energy to be ok with that. It was better to rely on ones self and find a way to explore life solo. Trying hard at that was a compulsion, just like taking the dog for an extra walk in case it was his last one.

Mum was about to turn 85. They told us eight years before that she didn't have long. I surmised that the day of reckoning would never arrive; I felt calmer. Rather than plan for the day, I knew I would plan for it when it happened. That thought felt better. And it was the same with the children. I would enjoy them until they flew the nest. But for them to mentally leave the nest but physically still be present was like a knife turning.

"Just making the most of things," was the reply to me being

a typical mum and remarking on tired eyes. I knew not to comment again. And I worked hard on not commenting.

Eating alone or with new friends who were really strangers, was ok with me. I was that girl who would usually walk into a room with a strut and a hair flick. I truly didn't mind. But I wanted to know someone cared if I lived or died. Was I unforgettable? Sometimes I would think of my funeral and loads of people standing at the back saying, 'I wonder if she knew how much of an inspiration she is to me,' and other such words.

I didn't doubt that was the truth. But accepting it, and sensing that other people could see what I saw in me was difficult for me.

Disneyland was a great time for family photos, but not when I was stood next to Tinkerbell. I was a size 14 dress, below average, and Tinkerbell was the size of a six year old child. Dad remarked how huge I was. I knew I wasn't, so why did the comment hurt me? Why did I let rejection or disapproval into my reality, when I knew I was a good human with a warm heart? I had my own back, over and over. I was a great person, and fabulous company. I was funny and clever and a little bit sexy in the right hands. Total faith in myself was ever present, but I was always on alert for the Tinkerbell comments.

My children wouldn't be purposely hurtful, of course. But they might find a person who would seem more awesome than me. There was room for us all, I told them. But when you check out, you check out.

177

29

Guys

They say the first cut is the deepest, and I am inclined to agree. You may have never experienced anything quite like it. Falling in love feels hard at first, and you know no one in the world could have ever felt like you two do. Then something happens, and he hurts you. He leaves. He puts a record on the record player with a song titled, "Je ne say par pourquoi," which is unhelpful. Of course, he knows why, he just doesn't want to admit it. Then you forget to eat; you watch the window hoping he will return, you wish you hadn't forgotten about your friends and you feel broken into pieces.

Picking yourself up gives you the feeling of strength which you never knew was there, and you congratulate yourself. Doing it once is enough. Putting yourself back together again time after time isn't easy.

Turning 50, I was happy enough as a single woman. It had become easier. That barbed wire around the heart was surely under lock and key. Apparently not. I gave to someone new as if it was the first time again, and now he was gone too.

I had given up and I'd decided to accept life flying solo.

Which was perfectly fine. I just needed a few tools in the box to navigate single life. I needed some plans. Plane tickets usually helped. Running shoes, both literal and metaphorical, to run when things felt difficult in a world of one. More often, this was a good thing. Knowing the hurt would be void made life easier to navigate. Planning for the future on a practical level was easier to control when there is one of you to plan, make things happen, budget, earn, sleep, hug.

Relying on oneself seemed like a logical step when there had been so many scars created. Healing was possible to a level but scars never healed completely and having a shoulder to lean on when bad days happened, was a pipe dream.

I was alone, but I was so full of gratitude and love for my children. But soon they would leave and then what?

30

Smile please

Photo opportunities presented themselves on every corner, and the street in between. Bangkok was fascinating. Glimmers of gold on the rooftops, on temples, statues and little tiny trinkets in the room were illuminating. This was an interesting city, for certain. The sky began to empty the clouds as we walked back to our hotel and I saw rain just like the storm in Koh Samui. We were getting soaked. Ahead of me, Jasmine walked with her friend under an umbrella. I was slow. My 90p rubber flip-flops from Primark were sliding around under my feet and I knew it would be easier to take them off. I was wondering what might be on the floor. Was there glass or needles? I kept them on and tried to keep my head down to shy away from the rain, but to keep walking.

"Come on, I've got you, take my hand," a guy friend said. I forced my hand out of his and said I was ok. I carried on walking. Lifting my head just enough to see under my fringe, I looked ahead. Jasmine was getting further away as we began to head into an opening between the buildings. I followed my feet, clutching at my flip flops between my toes, hoping this was still the right direction.

With every step, I felt I would be left behind. I could only see one person in front, and I didn't want to be too close to him for fear of giving something I wasn't giving. Rare occasions saw me wanting to be close to a man; this was not one of them.

Ahead, the opening was as dark as the wet night sky. It was impossible to see what lay in the alleyway but I continued to walk. We knew Koh Samui was safe. I hadn't heard enough about Bangkok so far but the longer I took to walk, the more I would get soaked. How far were we from the hotel? I lost the concept of time and place and I felt emotionally hurt inside my body. The rain pummelled its way through my favourite dress and onto my skin. Warm air prevented a chill on my body. My hair looked like I was freshly out of the shower. The ground got darker as I walked, one pink flip-flop in front of the other.

Passing through the blackened walls, I could hear a dog barking. The bark was a low tone and I knew there would be a bog dog the other side of the alley. Even though the alley opened into a wider gap, with some small shops within a square, it remained inky dark. The barking continued and I saw several dogs lounging on the floor, ignoring the rain. Oil formed under the raindrops as the smell of street food flooded my nose. Afraid of slipping, I slowed down. No one was in front of me. I had no capacity for fear.

The black,

the oil,

the dogs,

the unknown crime rates,

the invisible friends,

I kept walking.

Anger and sadness battled for my emotions. I saw an opening in the square and realised we were almost back into China Town, with red on every corner and beeping tuk tuks creating the craze and busyness.

"Smile Lou. Lou." A camera was pointed at me and I poked my tongue into the side of my cheek to make a bump and gave a peace sign with my left hand. Comedy escaped me inside, but I would mask, just enough, to help people think I was ok. I convinced no one. My fringe dripped salty rain onto my face and I brushed it aside to realise we were back in the entrance to our hotel.

The umbrella was lowered and Jas continued to laugh with her friend.

"You didn't even look back," I said, and instantly wished I didn't.

"I did. And I just had my camera, that's all. I didn't know how much rain it could stand."

31

Cities

Bangkok hadn't captured my heart. It was a fascinating place but it was full of traffic and dust and noise. Chaos. There was so much negative energy whipping around this city, and I was unsure about my mood.

Parts of the hotel looked incredibly interesting, a palette of colours inspired by an artist, I was sure. Soft furnishings welcomed late night chats from friends and efficient air conditioning allowed for solid sleep within non dancing hours. Love flowed for almost all of them, and I was thankful for the deeper connections we were forming. But aside of those positives I felt an air of unease within this city.

Early morning came and went. A breakfast full of dim sum and coconut sweets was on offer. The just-cooked omelette took my eye once again. My gut was behaving well and I decided to follow the path further into health and if eating eggs was what I needed to do, then so be it.

Further into the lunchtime rush, just before we were heading off to board the long tail boats for a river tour, I spotted Evan standing at the back of the crowd, facing the same way as them. He seemed to be looking at the ceiling as if he was studying the architecture. His gaze caught my attention for a while as, like dominoes, we lined up according to our level of agreement with the city. The group were first, then Evan. I stood behind him, watching his inner artist take a moment to breathe while this crazy city buzzed, like electric, all around us all.

After what felt like some very long moments, I walked up to him with ease and laid my hand on his shoulder with care,

"Hey, are you," he turned around to look at me and rested his hand upon mine as it rested on his shoulder, "a creative by any chance?" Evan smiled at me and turned square on to my body. His eyes half closed in a soft, knowing expression. We could see each other.

"Yeah."

"Thought so, I recognise that."

"I'm a designer."

" How are you finding it here?"

"It's a lot."

"Isn't it!" I rolled my eyes and sighed in relief at the same time. "I'd love to find a quiet coffee shop somewhere and write."

"Oh I'd love a coffee." We agreed we would find a coffee shop and talk about overwhelm, being a creative, and understanding the rhythm of a city such as this. It was upsetting our creative energies. Thank Goodness someone else understood. I wasn't going crazy. It was just our sensitivities. I was so thankful for Evan then and I wanted to chat more with him about our struggles in Bangkok, but a sharp voice ahead was calling us to head to the long tail boats. I already felt as if I had a warrior companion to glide across this journey with and the warmth filled me inside. Coffee shops were always one of my favourite things, but now, I could share a moment with another creative, and discuss the struggles we were facing. I couldn't stop the excitement within me. When would this happen? All through the rivers of Bangkok, the idea passed through my mind more times than I felt it should. Trying to focus on the flipping fish we were feeding at the side of the river, I aimed to be present. Temples were next and it was easy to focus on the huge golden Buddha called Wat Pak Nam.

"Behind there is a temple, you will want to see, it's worth going up to the top. Shoes off, shoulders and knees covered please." Our guide was not wrong. At the top of the temple, we stood behind the shoulders of the big golden Buddha and inside the building was an array of awe-inspiring brightness. I puffed as I aimed to catch my breath. There were many steps and we had to move at more than one step at a time, ideally. My daughter was ahead of me, also sweating but looking less dishevelled than I was. I was pleased she pushed for us to climb the stairs, despite not having much time before we needed to board the boat once again. The architecture was incredible. Over looking the Buddhas shoulders was the most worthy cityscape I have seen. There were no other words to describe this except 'city scape' as it was exactly as you would imagine. Bangkok seemed flat and the view across the city stretched to the horizon. Sky scrapers failed to mimic New York as both cities were in a league of their own. Racing to capture as many photos as we could, Jas and I took turns in facing towards the buddha for a shot of the back of our heads and shoulders, initially my idea. I didn't really see anything attractive in showing my puffy, red, wet cheeks. But my outfit was working well for me, with a slight flash of leg here and there between the slit in my wrap around skirt. I bought it instantly, knowing it would be a great fit because its pattern was covered in palm tree leaves. The sheer white shirt was tied up around my small waist (which was still small, despite menopause.) I worked hard on keeping fit and slim. The photos were good enough to post online. I hoped there might be some decent ones from the indoors. A passer by asked if we wanted a photo taken, as I was pointing my camera high in the air to get my best angle. We had to say yes and be thankful, but I knew I would prefer the selfie. Although I didn't like my profile, the picture captured the room behind us which was alive with the brightest grass green pattern on the ceiling which seemed to be lit by the pointed temple statue below it. The statue had lotus flowers lit up around its base. The ceiling seemed to make an illusion of a dome shape and there were pictures of meditating buddhas surrounding the bottom of the dome. Golden pillars met the roof, drawing attention to the cranky old trees floating out from behind the Buddha pictures. The detail was exquisite in this room and the temple seemed to be protected by ice-coloured blue glass dragons or sea serpents with a swan-like beak. Lined like soldiers, they were protected by a glass shield and an acrylic sign saying 'Do Not Throw Coin' which looked considerably out of place. Our bare feet felt cooler on the marble floor and I decided I was right about being happy in bare feet.

32

Sook

The boat travelled at speed, showering me in tiny droplets of river water, which was a worry and a delight at the same time. This was the final stretch of sailing we would do for the day as we docked in the bay of the Icon Siam. Our skipper used the length of her leg to stretch the rudder with her bare foot, to turn the long boat. She was strong. She was older than me. She looked weathered, but a certain joy seemed to accompany her furiosity at parking the boat.

A wide building stretched overlooking the river, looking as if it belonged on London Southbank, except there were cascading plants covering the front of the building. I had no idea what was next. But I heard the word Sook being mentioned. As if I was a sheep, I followed our friends past a Tiffany shop, and a Porche shop which housed some delightful cars. More plants draped from the ceilings between the shops and water features surrounded the outside edges of the pathways. Still a nutritionist at heart, despite me hoping to keep my attentions on writing, I spotted "Dear Tummy – Foods Market" in red and white neon signs.

The Sook was in fact an indoor food market with a delightful choice of many different foods. We passed underneath the sign saying "Sook Siam" and the air was filled with scents of many different types of cooking. Local people ate there. We had researched prior to coming, and we were told this was a good sign. Most of our group seemed to have visited there before. This was my trip of a lifetime and I wondered how people lived such a life. That little girl was still in there, watching every penny and believing things like this were not for people like us.

My eyes were largely drawn to the fresh young coconuts, which were my new favourite thing. I felt as though I was taking great care of myself by eating such foods. My gut would love me for that. The servers all wore masks. Some wore rubber gloves as they shaved the outer shell from the coconut piece by piece so that fussy people would be able to just eat the flesh without scooping it.

The sook was busy and chaotic with a plethora of colours scattered around. I walked around and around and double backed on myself looking for a safe food. I saw some BBQ meat which looked like it could be ok. I got nervous. I saw the rest of our group buying noodles and soup. Not a chance I would eat that. They all sat by a green baize stage with live music playing. A drummer tapped his sticks on what looked like an iPad and used his foot as if there was a base drum in front of it. Next to him was someone playing a Spanish guitar in total contrast. They smiled as they sang, and I told the rest of my group I would be back. They all sat eating while I did another lap of the food stalls before deciding to order another mango sticky rice with a twist. The outside of the coconut was shaped into a circular but upright shell; to act as a bowl and they scraped a ball of coconut on top as if it were ice cream. You could choose three fillings, and I opted for peanuts, mango and lychees. I was happy and potentially safe.

"Come on, let's move up to find Lou some space," one of our older friends said as I rejoined them.

"Oh thank you. Are you sure? I can perch on the end of the stage."

33

Darling

Walking around the shops seemed pointless to me. My back was hurting and the only thing I needed to buy was some face cleanser. There was no Superdrug in sight so I told Jas and her friend to go off without me. I had a phone signal, so I would find somewhere to sit and find them later.

My musical ears followed the sound of music past the Versace shop and into a blue-lighted clearing in the middle of the shopping centre. Three people sat lazily on the stage, singing acoustic sets of a song I'd never heard before. This was a delight to me, and I was overjoyed to sit there and lose myself in the notes as the lady sat and sang, tapping her thigh.

Something felt off. I wasn't sure if it was just me, or something else. I sat, stretched my back, enjoyed the air conditioning and decided not to think.

Much later, dancing followed back at the hotel and I was exhausted enough to excuse myself for the rest of the day. Before long, it was time to explore again the next morning, and I failed to keep up with the girls as they walked at speed for a couple of miles.

We were heading to the reclining Buddha, which was an iconic attraction. Time after time, we heard more about the significance of temples, and this huge Buddha seemed to put it to the test to be one of the most impressive sights there was. They just kept building more to outdo each other, over and over. This a concept I could relate to, as I strived within life to be the best I could be, until I heard about the law of attraction. The point of life was joy. A brand new concept which was sent to me while I sat in the Red Sea some years before. It confused the life out of me and I had been busy believing life was a terrible thing which we needed to white knuckle ride to death. Did we need bigger statues? Why did we find it important? Was there some other reason? I was starting to wonder if my symbols were already big enough, and the next step was joy.

Outside the building which housed the reclining Buddha was a gong as tall as me. I had tried to find things to add to my bucket list, to give me reasons to carry on, and banging a gong was one of them. The centre of the gong was a Sun, and that's the bit you would bang. The gold had chipped off to make black marks, but the top of the sun had a Chinese-looking protector guide holding a sword. On either side of him were dragons with heads made of fire. Underneath was blue, signifying water, with some tulip-type flowers flowing upwards. I didn't know what this all meant, but I found the coins I needed, put them in the donation box and picked up the mallet.

"Ready?" I called out to Jasmine, feeling as though I may have been spoiling her day. She nodded and held the camera in position. I used all my might to bang the gong as hard as I could. A quiet, but deep vibration emitted into the air. It was an anti climax but it showed that sometimes volume doesn't matter, so long as there is energy, there can be vibration.

197

34

Gatsby

That night it was fancy dress. One of my least favourite things. I was fussy when it came to such things. It was impossible to find something to fit the Great Gatsby theme when you were not seven stone and you also have a history of being equivalent to 47 weeks pregnant. I needed something to cover my tummy and the dress I had bought would have to be good enough as the waif like ladies swanned around with their figure clinging dresses.

Everyone took turns on the photo booth. If I didn't stand there, I would have looked silly. So I stood there, with my arms in front of me, like a small girl would. I tilted my head to the side and half smiled.

"They will be printed over there in a minute," the photographer said to me. I thanked him, and put the fake chalk sign saying 'Bangkok Baby' back in the box. I saw the photos land at the printer tray. I swallowed and put my glass of coke to one side and picked up the photos with my thumb and forefinger as if they were still printed wet, like they used to do. I looked down at the pictures. There were four of them on one sheet. The one holding the sign was the best. My fringe was shiny and smooth and my edge of my breast sat in perfect alignment with the pearls on the front of the dress. My shape looked good. My head was tilted just enough to let my long earrings fall with the pull of gravity and my half smile was convincing. The feather in my hair added to the effort of the Gatsby theme and I wondered if, for a woman in her 50s, I might have looked quite pretty.

I watched my friends bundle into the photo booth, climbing over each other and giggling as they fought for the props the photographer had brought. They were having a fantastic time. I looked down and my photos once again and decided I would take them back to the room so they didn't get spoilt.

Pushing the button for the lift gave me a slight electric shock and there was an instant 'ting' as the lift arrived. It was full of more than ten friends.

"Oh,"

"Lou, Lou, get in. Get in. Quick." Evan called out. I squeezed into the lift and laughed loudly as we all did.

"How many dancers can you get in a lift?" Charles called out as he smoothed his beard as if he was thinking.

"Hey, hey, let's take a photo!" And he did. It was the funniest photo I had seen and I was overjoyed that it ended up on Facebook, with a tag of me too. A wonderful and funny moment with my friends was recorded forever.

35

Striped bag

Breakfast was early for me. I wasn't sure I even wanted company but I was glad to see a seat in the window beckon to me. I was able to watch the street below. A man sat at the side of the pavement with his eyes closed. His hands sat as fists at the side of his head, cuddled into his temples, holding his tired head up. He had a large green waterproof bag and another stripy bag at the other side of him, with an umbrella propped on top of it. I wondered if he was homeless. He looked fairly clean and tidy, so I couldn't be sure. But I sat and sipped my coffee, giving a thought to the people who were homeless out there, or who had no family or friends. I gave myself a silent talking to as I wondered why I was so upset so often. I had no reason, not really. But in my reality, I felt as if life was too difficult at times and I found things hard. I had always wished it was different. Especially as a little girl when I used to try and describe a feeling I had as, "I have got that silly feeling again. I feel silly."

To this day, I don't know what that is. But it still comes to torment me at times. If I could brush that aside, people would think I was awesome.

My phone set off a ding and it was Sonia, inviting me to join them as they visited the Golden Palace. I had heard about the place and apparently, it was a sight to see. Immediately I replied with a 'yes' and began to work on excitement in place of anxiety for riding a Tuk Tuk, as she suggested.

We needed two Tuk Tuks as there were six of us riding to the palace. My friends allowed me to sit in the middle as I told them, "I'm such a scaredy cat," and we all laughed. It was true. I got more afraid of things as I got older, and I didn't want to fall out of a Tuk Tuk in Bangkok. Wedged in tightly, the drivers decided to race each other, to our delight. We squealed like children and my tummy began to hurt with laughter.

Within the palace, there was glimmering gold everywhere I looked. The sun shone off the buildings and the heat became unbearable. There was no wind and we were all soaked through with sweat. I branched off to wander by myself and typed in the group chat that I would get a cab back soon. Cabs were so cheap and I was finding this level of heat impossible. One of the others in our group sent an alarming message. She had a severe blood pressure drop and was trying to get some water and shade, but she had no money. I bought her some water and found her, struggling in the shade. She barely had the strength to say thankyou. I wondered if I was being too much, but decided to just go home.

36

Rooftop

It was time for the rooftop party. The party I was most excited for.

As it was time to leave our hotel, the rain started to fall from the sky as if there was no way of stopping it.

"There is a plan B. We can use the bar area which is inside," the group leader announced. I aimed not to respond to anything for fear of her sharp tongue and I just followed the group into our various mini busses. We arrived at the Marriott Hotel which was a luxuriously built hotel, and we had been instructed the dress code was chic rooftop vibes and no flip flops. I wore a new cheap dress which I had ordered online. I wasn't convinced it didn't have Grandma vibes, with the flowery pattern. It had looked cute on the model, but it was the best I could do, to wear with my trainers.

A cute blush of slight sun exposure was giving me a healthy glow which also had guilt attached. I was told to keep out of the sun since my skin cancer, two years before. The flushing cheeks helped to mask the chaos which was making its way into my head. This bar was chaotic and dinner was being served to all the wrong people, after a very long wait. After two hours, we were told we could head to the rooftop as the rain was slowing down. I waited until the rush had gone before heading up there. Jasmine had already been there and enjoyed a nice time with her friends while I took a minute to scroll on my phone and be quiet, I was the only one left downstairs.

Deciding to try and find the rooftop, I walked towards the lifts after twenty minutes of solitude. I met some others coming out of the lift who said they were going back up. At the top, Jas was there and said she would show us the way. She was beaming and seemed so happy as she raced up the last steps from the lift to the rooftop. I was about four people behind her as she fell on the steps. I heard a gasp.

Her name was called out by several people.

Except me.

She laid on the floor for a moment before trying to get up.

People were still making sounds.

I wanted to rush forwards, parting the crowd and pulling my little girl up and brushing off her grazed knee and hugging her, helping her to feel better just by showing her my love.

I stayed behind, silent.

"S'ok, I'm ok," she said as she started to pull herself up to her feet. She checked her knee and said it was ok. It wasn't. The bruise lasted for many days. My heart hurt as I tried not to look or fuss. Must be cool.

My heart hurt.

37

Vietnam

Waking next to the purple walls didn't get bothersome, but I was ready to move onwards to the island life once again. The alarm woke me and I hurried to shower, pack and get to breakfast in the hope of sitting in the window for a lazy half hour over my coffee ritual.

Thrilled to see they were still offering omlettes, I stood next to the tall man in front of me with my plate in my hand, watching the chef skillfully add whisked up egg to the pan. Never witnessing anything quite like this before, the speed assumed we had all day to eat our eggs. He tipped the pan to one side until it formed a crust. When it was slightly solid, he turned it, ensuring the egg was was a UFO shaped omelette. The pan remained tilted for the entire cooking session and after just a couple of short minutes, and a flick of the wrist, the food was on the plate. I was glad the eggs were runny inside. My digestion found it much easier. Cheese in the mix helped even more.

As a child, or rather, as a pre-Crohns patient, I had never eaten eggs or cheese. I simply didn't like food like that. But my research had shown me this was a game changer, and I learned to eat food which I had previously grimaced at.

Sitting in the window with my food, I was glad I had experienced Bangkok. There was so much to see. So much history was woven through this eclectic place. But I was one of the first to wait in line for the minibuses to take us to the airport.

Some friends were staying in Bangkok, some were flying to another part of Thailand, but many of us were flying to a little island called Phu Quoc, which belonged to Vietnam. Saying goodbye was never easy, but everyone had their agenda for making the most from being on the other side of the world.

Most of us were at least heading to the airport once again. An airport I felt I knew well, Bangkok was colourful as always and when I spotted a take-away mango sticky rice pot, I decided to buy it in case there was no gluten free food nearby in the next few hours.

Astro turf lined the area at the airport gate where the plane was leaving for Phu Quoc and this meant there was a wide open space. One of the incredible, chiselled bodied friends in our group decided we all needed to stretch, and commanded a yoga session. She expertly navigated us; we needed it. More photos followed as we all posted our fun times to Instagram as if it was all sunshine and rainbows.

The short plane ride to the Vietnamese island was fun, comfy and full of hope for my warm, cosy feeling once again. I wasn't sure I would feel the joy I had in Koh Samui, as time felt different. Perhaps there would be something similar to the indescribable feeling of a home for my spirit to rejoice in.

Stepping outside onto Vietnamese soil for the first time, I noticed the streets lined with coconut trees once again. Blue sky was broken with fluffy white clouds. Gentle breeze made an effort to cool us down as we continued to perspire while we waited for the transfer buses.

The hotel wasn't far away from the airport and we took it in turns to use the buses. I didn't mind waiting. The view in front of me was delightful enough to prevent boredom while we waited. I was happy to look at the trees all day long. Wandering across the road to take some photos, I couldn't stop the gasps; that familiar feeling engulfed me once again. Island life seemed to suit me so much better than city vibes.

Our group chat set off a ping, and we all checked our phones. One of our friends had already arrived in the hotel. She simply wrote,

Just you wait

38

Dreamland

She was right. This new hotel was incredible. I wondered if this was the best hotel I had ever stayed in. I'd seen some fabulous hotels over the course of my career, but this place was outstanding.

The swimming pool was an infinity pool with a backdrop of the beach, the sea, and more coconut trees. The restaurants served incredible food, and we met the Maitre d'hotel who introduced herself as Kate. I pictured a memory of Princess Katherine to help me remember her name, as I knew I would need to speak to her about the gluten free options. Soon after speaking to the staff dealing with food, it was time to check in to our rooms.

Welcome drinks were served to us as we completed the usual paperwork and gave over our passports to be copied. The drinks were purple, and the straws were made of a natural leaf; my favourite colour had me attaching this new leg of our journey as 'a sign'. We continued to enjoy our drinks as we headed up into the room. A man helped us with our cases. As he tapped the fob, he opened the door so we could step inside first. Both Jasmine and I gasped at the room in front of us.

The fridge didn't look like a fridge, but rather it was covered in bamboo. On top of the circular bamboo fridge was a tray laid out with special teas and coffees. Inside the fridge were little cans of free drinks and some mini water bottles. The bed was huge, with green hues, and it turned out to be like sleeping in a cloud. The pillows and duvets were so soft and comfortable. There was a large bathtub in the room as well as a separate shower, separate toilet and some other fancy stuff like pure silk dressing gowns, a beach bag with towels in, and a torch. After becoming educated in this part of the world, I had to assume the torch was in case of power cuts.

A room to top all rooms, I was delighted to be in the hotel; I gave it the award for the best hotel I had ever stayed in.

Mealtimes were delightful. The staff mesmerised me at the speed of service which gave the illusion of being slow and graceful, when in fact it was superfast. They were beautiful humans. My affection for the aura carried by the people working there was apparent to me.

Breakfast time the next day, saw people from our group asking me questions about certain foods, and what to do about self service. I was always happy to help where possible, but in this instance, I didn't know the answer.

"Kate, can you help please?" I called out. My friend who was asking the questions turned to me and smiled.

"I love the way you know all about the food, as well as know the names of the staff and what you need to ask for," she sparkled, and I felt smart.

The mealtimes passing from breakfast, to lunch, to dinner reminded us this trip was passing too fast. Consiously, I tried hard to store away every memory. Every feeling at bedtime as the pillows folded around my neck, every moment in the warm swimming pool, every meal we had the pleasure of taking in slowly, and every conversation with newly bonded people all needed to be etched in my memory.

39

People

Richard sat at the edge of his sunbed cross legged. I gathered he was meditating.

Some hours later, we floated in the same swimming pool, near each other as we started chatting. We had spoken several times before, but the usual, 'hey how's it going,' type of conversations. This time, we got deep. My favourite types of conversations are those which discuss what makes us tick as individuals. What pleases us, and what makes us passionate about changing lives. He was interesting; we spoke further. A lot of backstories, I was nodding along as I understood his path of self development. I was still on my journey, which had begun sixteen years previous.

"Just the two kids then?"

"Yeah, just the twins. I wanted more. I wanted loads of kids but," I trailed off.

"Did you, yeah?"

"Ya, wasn't meant to be in this lifetime." I paused and shifted my feet from under the water as I bobbed around, "their Dad didn't stick around and no one else quite hit the spot."

"Oh. Eye," Richard nodded and looked into the water, "you don't really like to ask. You know, people's relationships." He proceeded to make it very clear he was in a solid place with his lady who wasn't on this trip, and it was nice to see someone so faithful.

Our conversation continued long enough that my fingers were wrinkled and I sat in the pool holding my hands above the water as if I was wearing rubber gloves, ready to deep dive into surgery.

"He always told me I would be a sad, lonely old woman,"

"Did he? That's rich, and not true."

"Yeah, well that was after I said he couldn't have the babies to sleep over. They were only six weeks, and I was still feeding them, so it was a no. And they didn't know him. He met them once at the day they came into the world and nothing between then and asking to have them. Me saying no, he just said: I would be a lonely old woman. Sometimes I wonder if he might be right." I wondered why I was telling a stranger all this.

"Take no notice sweetheart, he's a dick, clearly." I liked the sentiment, but people fell by the wayside more often than I would have liked, and sometimes other people came along to replace them, sometimes they didn't.

As it happened, this conversation had felt wholesome, and I was glad we chatted. He was a new man in our circle, and despite his confidence, I wanted to help him feel welcome. He seemed a little like me, happy with his own company. Much as I didn't want to crowd him, I was glad when he organised a night out and pinged it into the group chat. I had promised to go, even if no one else did. He was good company.

Twelve of us arrived in dribbles and even though the group chat said the place was 'nextdoor to the hotel' it was actually a fair few minutes walk up the street. We arrived to a bar with plastic seating out the front and as you entered the place, the floor was a smooth concrete, not much good for dancing on, but nothing ever stopped us. We would kick off our shoes and embrace it. The DJ was the owner of the bar, who had struck up a deal with Richard to stay open, play music and welcome us to dance after 11pm, when our own DJ stopped playing at the hotel. The owner looked a bit like Jason, but probably more sober, and he had a wide smile which seemed to light up in time of the beat of the music.

They had lit a fire close to the archery area, which I guessed was to keep the mosquitos away. We didn't need it for the heat. It was still 31 outside. We all still continued to sweat as we played archery, danced in little 'simon says' rounds, and got brought shot glasses with a pink fluid in. My mental health was improved for not drinking alcohol, to the point I was almost becoming afraid of it. Instead of drinking, I would take photos while they all drank, and likely wouldn't look like a wierdo for not joining in.

"Lou Lou, boomerang," Josie commanded as she mimicked filming with her hands. I took a boomerang and then I heard, "Go on Lou Lou," to encourage me to drink. I'm not sure what I replied but, "No it's ok, it's nice," was the reply.

After three hours of sheer fun, we all headed back to the

hotel. New friendships were formed and I was thankful for that special time, but it was time to sleep as there was a boat to catch the next morning.

215

40

Snorkels and sand banks

Several of our group decided to stay and relax in the hotel and forfeit the boat trip. I understood that. It was such a fabulous place to hang out. Without us there, it would be extra quiet.

After overriding the air con timer, I crept out of the bedroom, making sure I had all the things I needed for the day. Jas would sleep more soundly with the cooler air in the room. It was still a little dark outside when I wandered down to breakfast for an oval omelette and a coffee. I didn't want to overeat as the sea looked a little choppy. Seeing washed up jellyfish on the beach ensured I wouldn't be going in the water. I was never sure why I was more ballsy in the Red Sea with my new husband back then, but maybe I've just got more afraid. One thing I knew was my deep desire for seeing the lush hills beside the water which Vietnam was famous for.

Climbing aboard the boat, I notice the silver tanks glistening. Divers were surely taking the plunge. This was something I had never seen before and I was excited to be on the boat, taking photos and videos for my friends, and enjoying the peace and quiet you occasionally feel on a boat.

Within minutes, we were leaving the port and taking to the sea, passing fishing boats which look like a boat you might see on a painting of the local sea. Five minutes more and I got to see exactly what I had wanted to see when I decided to book the extra trip to Vietnam. Lush green hills framed the sea, interrupting the blues of the sky and the water.

Standing on the top deck of the boat, I was smiling by myself as I saw a floating deck, with a house built out of old wood and corrugated iron. There was an outbuilding which seemed to be where the oil drums were stored. A man punted up to the deck, standing on a flat boat. He seemed to be delivering drums of water, to the annoyance of a dog who also seemed to be living on the deck. The barking sound echoed through the hum of our boat as we sailed past.

Five minutes of plain sailing passed when I noticed the sound of the engine roaring. I looked to the back of the boat and the wake seemed to catch my eye. An older lady called over to me, "Oh that doesn't look good does it? What's that?" She pointed to the back of the boat.

"No I think it's just the wake."

Then we heard, "everyone, everyone," and we were being called to stand at the front of the boat. Friends from below climbed up the stairs to the top deck and joined in the laughter we were creating. None of us really knew what was happening, but we knew it was a good photo opportunity. We called down to the crew below and all smiled and waved to the camera. The boat was a turquoise colour in contrast to the bright blue sky above, and our outfits messed up the theme entirely. We spent a lot of time laughing as we stood at the front of the boat. Something fun was happeneing.

One hour later, we felt sick. The hum of the angry engine was a nauseating sound, and the rocking motion of the boat was made worse by the fact we were stuck on a sandbank.

The staff had called us to stand at the front of the boat, hoping our collective weight may help to lift the tail of the boat enough that we would free ourselves of the bank. It didn't feel like a worrying time. Then we were called to the bottom of the boat, and instructed to stand at the front. We walked past discarded yellow towels, draped over the inside seats. Our strewn bags perched on the tables. One staff member was looking over the side of the boat as it rocked. Our friend spent the time in the toilet, throwing up. He was sure he had a tummy bug.

After a while, the crew told us to go and sit back down. My back clicked in several places as I sat and I tried not to let it show on my face. I was no good at standing still for periods of time. We sat, waiting. I looked up at the life jackets. I pictured an out board motor and assumed it had propellors. What if one of them was caught in the sandbank and was powerful enough to turn over the boat? I felt calm as I began to realise this was worrying enough to figure out a plan. Sat next to Richard, I knew he was an experienced diver as he was diving before we even left London, and sharing photos and videos of tiger sharks in the group chat.

"Do you think we need to worry? There's not enough life jackets there for everyone. Should we check who might need one and who's a stronger swimmer?"

"God, Lou, you sound like a spy," he smiled at me and looked into my worried eyes, "no, we are just stuck on a sandbank that's all. Worst thing, we will have to stay here until the tide comes back up. That will be about, erm, 8 hours."

How much drinking water did we have? Was there everything onboard for everyone to survive eight hours? There was no phone signal at all, despite my ESim. The people back at the hotel would be worried. How would they know we were ok? How would they know what was happening? I swallowed hard and the sticky throat didn't help me to remain calm. I became worried. The staff moved swiftly through the boat from the engine room in the middle of the boat, to the bow and back again, before they began calling something out.

"Don't they have a radio?" I asked Richard, who just laughed through his nose.

Two of the crew removed their T-shirts and started to wave them in the air. The front of the boat was alive with people and boats driving past in the distance were ignoring us. They cruised on past as our crew called out, whistled and continued to wave their t shirts. The blue water reflected the sunshine as a tiny tug came to help us. One of our crew gathered up a rope, threw his t shirt over his shoulder and bent at the knees, where his avocado pattered shorts stopped. Our friends were making jokes about throwing the rope and missing, the tug being too small to pull us and other unwelcome notions which didn't help my anxious thoughts. "A great story, it makes a great story," I said with a fake laugh. I wished I hadn't gone on the trip. I could have stayed and relaxed back at the hotel with the others.

The little blue tug looked like a fishing boat from the film Mamma Mia, and the solitary crew member on board caught the rope as it was thrown.

"Back in, Back in!" our crew commanded. We moved too slow and they began to shout. "To the side, to the side. The side, the side!" Chaos began and panic was very present. I took a seat at the side. One of our annoying group had been complaining all day and he was just standing in the middle of the seats. "Sir! Please sir!" He was waved to the end and I tried to keep my camera rolling to capture this exciting and worrying time; for the story.

"What's this for?" I asked Richard.

"If they are pulling us, and the rope snaps, it will whip someone. All sorts could happen. It's dangerous, but it'll be ok." He knew everything.

The crew member with the avocado shorts was tying the rope at our end, he was sweating and his triceps were glistening as he moved. The boat was still rocking so much, he would periodically stumble and need to hold on to the side of the boat.

Taking up the slack of the rope, the little blue boat looked as if it would tip as it heaved to get us off the sandbank. The smell of fuel was becoming overpowering but it needed one last rev to help the tiny tug. Cheers erupted, and I guessed we were free. The small and might tug had set us free after being sat there for hours and as if nothing happened, our boat just carried on forwards.

Passing underneath a long cable car trail, connecting to a huge water park on Thom Island, I knew I should take photos as it was the worlds longest 3 wire cable car with a length of 7899.9m. Soon after, the anchor was lowered and our friends took to the sea. People of all ages, shapes and sizes and swimming abilities went in. I found a hammock type of seat and decided to let the sun kiss my skin slightly.

When they came out of the sea, a few of them said they had seen something on the bed which was indescribable. "It's kind of like a load of carrier bags all strewn together, but it was brown and, oh, eww, I just didn't like it. I don't know what it was but it swam past James and he got straight out." Those people who had seen it, didn't enter the water for the next few dives. We still don't know what they saw on that day.

Our drama was soon forgotten as the crew still took us to the dive spots as if we hadn't been stuck on a sandbank for hours. The water calmed considerably at the final dive spot and some of the group decided to start jumping from the top of the boat. I admired them and started to wonder if I should begin pushing myself to do things I'm afraid of.

Back at the hotel, I ran through the reception area and went to find my daughter. She was casually laid on a sunbed, under the umberella.

"Hey," I called before I reached her.

"Hi. You ok Mum?" I sat on the sunbed next to her, with my towel draped around my shoulders.

"Oh God, you are not going to believe what happened. We had to be rescued."

"What?" she sat upright, "I did wonder if something went on, as time went by, I thought. Oh, are you ok?" I filled in the gaps before we climbed into the pool for happy hour and fresh young coconuts. The sky delighted us with visions of purple and pink as the sun went down.

223

Louise Usher

41

No Pizza

They called them TukTuks but they were like elongated Brum's. It got stressful trying to navigate how much we all needed to pay and there was too much maths involved.

Arriving at the pizza place, three of us were gluten free. Finding seats, when my anxiety was playing about, was making me feel uncomfortable. Jasmine knew this was her sign to take over, and she floated off without question, to ask about a gluten free menu. "No, no, none like that," she was told and she came back to two of us who were gluten free with heavy shoulders.

"They can't do gluten free," we looked at each other.

"Let's go, let's just go," our animated friend Lara said, as if this was inconvenient. As we began to leave, someone grabbed my arm.

"Ok Lou?"

"No gluten free," I rolled my eyes and carried on walking, trying to be okay. But I felt the experience was uneccesarily stressful for some reason, part of that reason being my mind.

Walking up the street, we were still certain we were safe to do that.

But I wondered how we will get back to the hotel. "Same way as we got here, Tuk Tuk," Lara said, and I knew from her tone, my mind was over active. Jasmine knew me well enough to know what I needed in these moments and she stepped up like a star.

"What about this place? This looks nice," Lara pointed to a menu outside of a restaurant and we began to flip through the plastic pages when a man came out to see if we needed any help. The two girls started asking about gluten free menus and the man looked blank and pointed to the various dishes on the menu in a 'draw a snake upon your back' fashion.

"Yes, but," Lara asked expressively, "do, you have, any Gluten Free?"

He pointed at the menu again, turned a page and began pointing to different dishes. "Oh come on," Lara suggested, "shall we just go back to the hotel and eat there?" We did.

Before we sat at a table, Richard text,

Where you at?

We have come back, Pizza place no good. Eating by the sea in the hotel. Welcome to join.

Might do, if that's ok.

He didn't. The girls and I had a typically girly night with sensitive chats, some tears and a loving conversation with a backdrop of the ocean sounds. The meal was excellent, well presented and I had a feeling this was a day in my history which would forever etch itself in my memory.

42

Salt Coffee

Rain hammered the decking near the pool as we walked to breakfast. "Miss Louise," Kate beckoned to me and continued walking as she held out her hand in a straight line. As if she had an invisible line from her fingertips to the table, we all walked in a line to the square wooden table, one row away from the window. Kate looked pleased with herself, but I was smiling back with a half-disappointed vibe. The window framed an incredible sight outside. The palm trees were struggling to keep upright against the winds, and the rain on the glass performed an intense echo through the restaurant. Outside, between the restaurant door and the pool, men were holding ladders for each other as the awning danced with the wind. Aiming to create a porchway, the men battled with the plastic sheets as their hats blew around their necks, attached to the string. Weather like this was so interesting to me. Excitement bubbled in my belly as I sat at the table for breakfast.

Another lesser-cooked omelette was my choice, as I wondered what the day ahead may look like. Jasmine was as clear as the raindrops when she verbalised, she was settled and happy spending time with her friends at the hotel, even if it wasn't swimming pool weather. Perhaps it was time for me to venture out for that coffee at last.

Did you get your coffee yet?

I sent a text to Evan who was in a different country. He didn't reply, but it felt comforting to think someone knew, and understood the need for the ritual of going for coffee. It wasn't the caffeine, the drink or the cup, it was the chink of time which was being carved, just for oneself. Time to be, and to file the thoughts into some tone of organisation rather than letting them muddle into an untangleable mess. I wondered if the rain and wind would calm down enough for me to venture out.

By 9.30am I was armed with a longer than average umbrella. It was time to leave the resort and over the road to the coffee shop which served salt coffee. My tote bag was firmly fixed to the little concave on my shoulder. Inside, my journal and pens sat neatly next to my glasses case. Pride filled me as I hoped someone would see the bag on my shoulder and the letters spelling out to the world that I had been to a publishing show. *Yes world, I am a writer, see this, and encourage me. I need a nudge and I'm not sure who might give that nudge to me.* My thoughts spoke to whoever could hear them. Reality had me knowing the little poke in the ribs needed to come from me. Only I could do it, and I wasn't sure when the time would be as perfect as it needed to be for me to fully launch that author career. So I straightened the shoulder straps and walked past the indoor fountain en route to the place where I could sit for a while and journal.

My phone was sideways on as I hit the record button. It was going to be a significant trip to the coffee shop and I wanted to vlog it all. Phoebe had done such an amazing job with her little short video. Inspired by her, I felt a need to taste the coffee and to mimic her video which had somehow struck a chord with me. Vlogging in public had become commonplace and I wasn't particularly shy about it at all. Still, I hoped the coffee shop would be quiet. I hadn't expected what I was about to witness in the form of what they considered a coffee shop.

My fringe dangled in my eyelashes. I was desperate to cut the fringe. Usually, this was a perfect frame of my face, but it had grown too long, and it was acting up, wanting its usual weekly trim. Clutching the umbrella, I tried to get it out of my eyes as well as keeping it straight. I could see in the camera lens just how frazzled I looked. It was the humidity. Otherwise, I was looking like an island life girl. Shell necklace, linen shirt, umbrella, backpack and a feeling of not being me, simply because I had not written with a pen since we left the UK. Stepping to the side of a green wheelie bin which had blown to the ground, I looked across the road to assess what might have been going on at the salt coffee place. It snugged into the middle of the mini-mart and a shanty shack made of tarpaulin which looked like somewhere they kept tubs of paint and discarded mopeds. Three green umbrellas, like ones you use for shade in the garden, kept the entranceway and blackboard dry. Healthy coconut trees assisted the creation of a roof, alongside another huge tree which looked like an overgrown rhododendron which you would find in the National Trust places in Torquay.

Tram Huong Chan Tam was printed above some Chinese writing on a shop sign. A yin and yang sign acted as a full stop at the end of the sign. The moment stood proudly as if this was a perfect holiday activity. I stopped to cross the road and wondered if the place was open. I hadn't considered how early in the morning it was.

A cart stood on wheels, with rocks as brakes, and propped up against it was a blackboard with yellow paint on it spelling:

Salt Coffee

Coconut Coffee

Egg Coffee

Fresh Coconuts

Smoothies

The fruit for the smoothies was sitting in the cart, all ready. I read the list and wondered what I would choose. Did it have to be salt coffee, like Phoebe? Sitting in the middle of a street in Hanoi, she was being beeped at as she recorded the tasting of the coffee. She seemed somehow more professional than me at creating a video. I didn't know why. She picked up a little doughnut type of dessert and asked, "Would that be disgusting to dip that in there?" and pointed to the salty cream on top of the coffee. I would omit the dessert, due to my gut, but I saw that she followed instructions from Chloe who said she shouldn't stir it up, but try a little of the cream first. At the end of her video, she gave it a 10/10 and that was good enough to convince me to opt for salt coffee.

Green baize lined the end of a concrete hill which I guessed was something I needed to go up. I spoke to the camera, "Oh there's a dog there, they are usually ok, but because, in case it's a guard dog, I just won't," and I stood reading the menu instead, figuring out how it was 35,000 Vietnamese dong to enjoy this coffee. That was less than £1.

As usual, a wonderful lady appeared in no time. I was sure they slept waiting for customers and never left. She tried to find me a dry chair underneath the cotton sheets which were draped just above head height from tree to tree. They caught the falling leaves and branches from the trees. Dirty as they looked, it was a cute backdrop for this place which looked like it was created for smaller humans; not quite dolls house size. More like infant school size, the chairs gave my back relief as I crunched up in the chair and pulled the small plastic table in front of me. Strings of lights were woven above my head in full size light bulbs. I wondered how cosy that must have looked at night time. It was a pity there wasn't time to come back again.

The lady who was serving me was running around, even though there was just me and the dog there. She had a cloth in one hand and fiddled with her hair in the other hand. I filmed the back of her head and spoke to the camera,

"this is perfect, it's so sweet the way they run off. I feel so so happy in this moment, this is perfect." I journaled, highlighting I had not written for eight days. I wrote: I think I have a new story.

My salt coffee arrived, and looked stunning in its glass container and steel spoon. The cream on top was thick, like slightly whipped cream and there was a paprika coloured sugar sprinkled on top. Just as I began filming, with a bright red face, the server brought some water to me.

"Gaman," I said and held my hands to prayer just under my chin. After a quick slide of my finger, to catch the dripping cream, I licked my finger and announced the taste was lush. Holding the straw between my thumb and finger, I took my first sip. The flavour was like salted caramel. Before I was tempted to drink any more, I posed for a selfie and realised how wet my face was. My fringe was stuck to my forehead, but this added to the aesthetic of my untamed curls and the trees behind me.

"Want me to take that for you?" I heard a familiar voice from far away and I put my phone into my lap the instant I heard the click. I closed my journal at the same time as looking towards the voice. It was an English voice but I needed my glasses to focus on who that was. I could see a tall figure at first and that was all. But it sounded like Dara.

"Of all the places, in all of the world," the voice trailed off. As he stepped closer, I could see a tidy short beard, cut close to the jawline. Dark eyebrows and neater-than-my hair helped to piece the puzzle together. I couldn't mistake his voice, public schoolboy perfect with a hint of banker from London, it was Dara. I sat silently. I just stayed sat.

"Hello Babe," he dipped his head under the drapes above and let out some sort of laugh from his nose, "been a while." He bent down and touched the end of my nose.

"What on Earth?" I breathed. Grinning, I moved the chair next to me, "this is kind of dry. And I recommend the salt coffee. Want to join?"

"Babe, I would love to join you. Been trying to join you for, what must it be now, over five years?"

"Well, yeah," I dipped my gaze towards my legs.

"Why though? I wanted to see you. Never mind. We have this coffee date now, after all."

"Yes, true. I fly to the next place tomorrow." I took away any expectations right away, just like I did before.

"Ok. It's ok, shh," he said as he looked into my eyes. Was he flirting? "I thought after the McDonalds, you would be sure to come back for more," he said and started laughing.

"Ha, there was nothing wrong with that date at all."

"I know, fun right." He waved to the lady who was on her way to take his order and then continued to dominate our conversation, "so why babe?"

"Why didn't I reply? Or why are we bumping into each other on the other side of the world?"

"I wanted to give things a shot," he said.
Back then, we would talk after work, for hours on end, night after night. I gathered he was bored and filling time, which I may have been doing too. I looked up at the drapes and said, "It's all you can do to duck under those," and tried to laugh. I/ didn't want to have

that conversation. I was trying to figure out if I was delighted to see him or annoyed that my moment to myself was taken. My time by myself was something I enjoyed because it was a safe place. Being next to boys had become uncomfortable after so much hurt.

Dara looked above his head at the drapes, "those? Well, I'm sitting down now," he grinned and looked into my eyes, "next to you." He held his gaze and I felt the familiar feeling in my stomach which had been absent for so long. I was desperate to break the stare but I also wanted to remember who I was there and then for a while. I buried that girl. Periodically, she wanted to climb back to the surface and be a part of a loving world, with joy and passion which revolved around love. Fear frequently stopped that; it was no wonder. Time and again I had trusted someone with my heart and time and again I endured hurt. I had felt safe with Dara, because my heart was not involved. There was never any question about us having a happy ever after. He wanted to have children. I couldn't give him that. There was one reason huge enough to keep my feelings at the edge of diving in, but there were other reasons too. Seeing Dara as nothing more than a gorgeous distraction gave me a sense of safety.

"Yes, you are." I let out a sigh. "This is the strangest thing isn't it."

Dara nodded and smiled so broadly; it was definitely a grin.

His coffee was on the way, and he spoke to the sweet waitress in fluent Vietnamese. I watched him, with my mouth open. She replied to him in the local language and they both had a full on conversation. As they finished talking, he turned to me with a failed attempt at an innocent look, "what?" he said and almost blew the cream off the top of his salt coffee with the air he blew out of his nose.

It was incredible to see him and I felt my body come alive while I sat next to him. I had folded away my journal and embraced our conversation about work. He updated mee on his career development and I felt pleased that he was doing so well in his job in the city. I'd been through the process with him as he finished his legal qualifications and landed his first major post with the bank. To see how far he had progressed in over five years was thought provoking. Who else do we lose touch with? How far have they come? Are they ok?

"What now Lou?" He asked.

"I'm just dodging raindrops today and possibly packing my case, remember, I'm off tomorrow."

"Shame. I have another five days here. I suggest we make the most of bumping into each other, shall we?" He looked at the end of my nose as I wrinkled my face with a quizzical expression. I wasn't sure, and I had a lot of questions. If I didn't spend more time in this moment, would I regret the decision?

"I, erm, I Dunno. Kinda. Yeah? What you thinking?"

"It's a bit early but maybe we can try and grab some food?" I surrendered and we were soon walking the main street together, hoping to find somewhere to eat some food. We chatted non stop and after a short while, we sat and enjoyed a rice- laden lunch which was served in a carved out pineapple shell. He listened to me. I watched his jaw moving as he ate while I spoke. Without any doubt, he was the most handsome man I had ever seen and I thought back to the night we first met in the flesh, after chatting online for so many months. Perhaps my childhood programming had given me some negative thoughts, perhaps I could blame the school bullies. Maybe the infidelities I had experienced were responsible for my feeling, but I knew back then there was no way Dara looked like his photos. I knew it was a cruel joke. Regardless I had always enjoyed our conversations and I was happy enough to keep talking. Seeing his photos online had me excited inside of my belly, and the fact he said the same of me too had me cautious. But when he asked to first meet me, I only hesitated for a slight moment. As long as I was careful, I didn't really think much could go wrong, but the joke would be over and I would go back to the girl I was in the past. The one who had just been diagnosed with AS. The woman who knew her disease would progress and possibly leave her body unable to embrace the desires inside. So I agreed to meet him.

My car is a big white one, an SUV

I text him, while hoping to impress.

Ok. Mine is the Audi Q8. A black one

His reply had me knowing this was completely a cruel joke. When I drove to the car park and saw a black Q8, my heart stopped for a second. No way.

He text again, once he saw my car.

Come over

Was I about to be murdered, or laughed at? Those were my ruthless days, when I was hoping to cram in all areas of life while I could, just in case. I felt like I knew him. We had chatted since forever, for hours, and my vibe was telling me I was ok, arguing with those battle scars.

You come over

I replied, knowing I would have more control if he was in my car. It was clean, after all. Not a kid's sticky sweet in sight.

He didn't reply, but in the dim lamplight, I could see a tall guy in a long dark coat getting out of the car. The back of his head looked tidy and I had to stop looking. I got nervous. I heard a click of the passenger door handle, and the door opened. When he sat in the seat, it I got to see his face, full on. It was him.

I gasped inside. He was handsome.

Nothing happened between us that night. He bought me a hot chocolate from McDonalds after I relented and got into his car and he drove us through the drive through. I had a rule not to eat on a first date. Even though this was the first 1st date I had in three years. Besides, looking at him while we spoke was enough.

"Where you drifted off to?" He asked.

"Honestly?" I giggled, "I was thinking about the first time I saw you."

"Yes? And?"

"I probably never told you this but I was sure your photos were a catfish."

He laughed hard, throwing his head back as his mouth opened and the veins on the side of his temples bulged.

"No way? You didn't?"

"Yes, well, come on, look at you," I was comfortable enough to confess.

"Babe, look at you," he said seriously as he leaned over the table and touched my chin with his thumb and finger, pinching me in a sweet torment. He meant that. I wanted to stay for longer. Dara reached behind his back, pulling his shorts away from the skin, "ugh, sweaty mess," he said as he stretched his body and looked for the waiting staff. "We need to get going babe," he said. I nodded and used bravery to bring myself back to the icy, non-feeling self.

Moments later, the bill was paid and he insisted on it being his treat once again. The fact that it cost less than we would have paid for two meals in McDonald's that previous night was irrelevant, it was a gesture. I pulled a bill from my purse to leave the tip on the table and I looked back up from my purse, hoping to not sigh as I said, "well, this has been an unexpected pleasure."

"It IS. Come on," he announced and took my hand towards the restaurant exit.

"Where we going?" I asked, hoping to mask my delight.

"For a paddle."

Within minutes, we were on the soft sand with our shoes off, walking back towards my hotel. I kicked off my flip flops and dangled them between my fingers. I refused to walk in the water. I had seen two washed up jellyfish and heard stories of people getting stung while we was on our boat trip.

"You can if you want but I'll stay this side."

"I'm not scared!" Dara laughed and reached out to me to ensure I was far enough away from the water but close enough to him so we could still chat, "You? You can stay there," he said as he took a hold of my hand on an outstretched arm. He held my hand, like a boyfriend would. I looked down at our hands as if they might explode. "Ok?" He asked and I nodded after a slight hesitation.

Safe conversation flowed as the skies above turned deeper grey and clouds rolled in. The chill of the rain could not be felt and I was sure we had some more time. I'd lost my sense of direction to the level of knowing I was heading towards my hotel, but I couldn't say how far away it was. Dara pointed to the line of coconut trees and dipped his chin in a questioning look. The sunlounges were laid underneath them, empty. The blue material outstretched, kept the accumulation of sand to a minimum and we started walking towards the loungers.

Dara sat himself close next to me on the same lounger and still held my hand. Previous history between us showed me I was comfortable with him and I had nothing to fear. Not much had changed, except my children were now grown ups. Looking at his face, I still remembered how I felt this was a joke but he had shown me over several years now that he had nothing but good intentions for me. We were two friends, who talked a lot and seemingly found each other attractive, yet never acted upon it.

"Babe, I have a question," he looked at my face as the sound of waves roared behind us. I nodded and knew this was going to be something serious.

"Why didn't anything happen between us?"

"Oh my god, what?" I shoved his shoulder playfully and let go of his hand, "you are not asking me that!"

"Seriously, I am."

"You know what the situation was. Like, you wanted a future I could not give you and all that. I couldn't get involved. Not fair on either of us, so it made sense to keep our distance."

"I get that. But I did want you. I want you to know that. I still haven't met someone I click with like I did with you. I wish there was that women who could have it all, but it seems she's just not out there."

"You'll find her. It's going to be ok. Lovely to see you, but," he cut me off. Dara took a hold of my hand again from where it was dangling between my legs, holding the edge of the sun lounger and he held my hand in unison with his gaze. He looked as if he was going to start moving towards my face and I studied his features so closely in such a short instance. He was moving towards my face. His scent got stronger. He continued to fix on my eyes until his eyes became a blur and I felt the end of his nose touch mine. We were going to kiss.

The brush of his lips on mine commanded them to react and we locked in an embrace for the seconds which passed. I was kissing Dara. The most handsome man I had ever seen was kissing me.

Sweetest kisses were exchanged between us for some time. He

skilfully navigated my willing face and showed me exactly what I had expected, he was one heck of a sexy guy.

He shuffled on the sun lounger and released my lips from his. He chuckled playfully and said, "Gonna have to stop," as he moved his shorts.

"God Lou, why didn't we make more of it back then?"

"You know why."

"Yeah but after that, you started pulling back, must have been about six years ago or something. Think it was just after you was in Bosnia on your writing thing. I sensed something happened." I took a deep breath.

"It did. I fell in love."

Dara had just kissed me. Me.

Me.

He kissed me.

What the heck? I hadn't wanted to speak about my ex lover at this time. The man I fell in love with could give me everything Dara couldn't. It wouldn't be fair to expect more from Dara or even to try and seduce him, even if I could. I had something pretty amazing to offer to the best guys and I needed to start accepting that. I was something special. He had just kissed me, and whenever I felt insecure, this was a memory I locked away to remind me just how desired I could be.

I released my hand from his and turned my shoulder to line up next to his. I cupped my hands over my nose and rubbed my face.

Air left my body and a sound hung in the air. I looked at the waves. Feelings inside my body were choosing to continue testing me as I told the woman in me to stay silent. Several years had passed since the woman had come out to play. It was safer this way. She was deep down inside, aiming to heal that little seven-year-old and neither of them had time for boys. Besides, there was mum to consider, and the twins, and paying too many mortgages, and focus was necessary. Except when music played and the body commanded to dance; then it was completely fine to let go and allow those worries to vanish, just for a while. But boys? They made things difficult. So why was there that feeling inside which was so hard to ignore? Emotions and biology, a scary mix which never allowed me the strength to keep a hold of what was sensible. Was sensible the right thing? I was never sure either way.

"Stunning isn't it," Dara nodded to the shore line which seemed illuminated by the dark gret clouds above.

"Love it. Perfect." I sighed again and looked down at a little bit of skin at the side of my thumbnail.

"Don't pick that!" Dara's eyes followed my gaze. He laughed within his mouth.

I took a deep breath and continued the conversation, "I would really rather not talk about him. It's in the past now. But things changed so quickly for me. And I couldn't be anything like whatever you wanted or needed." I wasn't trying to forget falling in love, but I hadn't fathomed what it was, what happened, and even if it was completely sealed shut. Speaking about what I had felt had the potential to uncover some of the hurt I had expertly buried. That was a risk I was not prepared to take and I finished the conversation with, "I would rather respect the memory than speak about it. It's just how I feel."

"Why won't you talk about it? I don't get it. He must have been something special to have stopped our contact." My eyes met his in a sideways glance, full of pain and sadness. I blinked slowly and looked back at him again. The gaze answered in a way which words couldn't. 'Something special' echoed through my heart and I blinked again before looking to the shore. I had taken significant time to fathom how to stop the hurt just enough for the world to keep turning, but while keeping a tiny invisible thread between us so I would never forget the memory of the man I was so in love with. Thinking about him again was taking my energy somewhere different from the place it was sixty minutes before as I began to write in my journal, with my salt coffee, alone.

Dara felt the energy and expertly bounced the conversation into a different shade.

"Girls are tough now, you know."

"Yep. Guys too. Is easier alone."

"You mean that?"

"I do. Easier."

"Is hard to find someone nice."

"True."

Dara took a breath and stretched his torso high above his hips and put his arms above his head in a fake yawn. "What about your daughter?"

"What about her? Is she single you mean?" I turned my neck so fast it clicked. My eyes left the heartbreak of hurt behind and widened so my eyelashes touched the top of my eyelids.

"Yeah. What about her?"

"Are you asking for you?" I almost bellowed as loudly as the crashing waves.

"Why not?"

"Oh. My God. You are disgusting." My reaction had no chance of being controlled or contained.

"Umm I'd imagine she's a nice girl, like her Mum, so maybe?"

"Noone wants relationships anymore. People are waking up and realising they are difficult. She doesn't want a relationship either Oh Man… that's really sick and twisted. I can't believe you said that." I crossed my arms in front of me and shifted so my leg wasn't touching his.

"You asked!"

"You shouldn't have even thought that."

"Why would you ask that and prompt me?"

"I didn't prompt you. You asked!"

"You asked."

"I think you should go." I stayed sitting down despite my body wanting to move. I wanted to be back on my own again.

"Come on. Lou. Look this is fine."

"Go." I looked into his eyes. The beauty had gone. They were still dark, his lashes were still long, his jaw still at a right angle to his neck and the veins still pulsing. But there was a black hole where desire was. One question can undo those emotions.

I picked up my bag and put it on the lounger, next to my thigh so he could get out easier. I remained silent but continued to look at the sand beneath my bag. Dara knew that was his que and stood up, straightening his shorts which were stuck to him. "Look, I'm sorry," he said as if he couldn't understand why I was so upset. Refusing to look up, I moved my knee for him to walk past and fixed my gaze at the sand in a constant stare. Every cell within me wanted to sit alone and ponder all that happened as he took one slow step after the other, as if I was going to call after him.

A chocolate box of emotions unfolded as he walked further away. I had felt attractive and desired by the most handsome man I felt I had seen at the end of my kisses in a long time, and that seemed huge. I needed to process those emotions and begin to realise that not only was I a kind person who wanted the best for others, but maybe I looked ok too. He was clearly into me in a physical sense and after my brother-in-law told me, back in the 80s that his brother could do better, I hadn't been my best cheerleader. The mirror had never shown me anything ugly, but it hadn't shown me a reflection of utter beauty, worthy of someone who looked like Dara. How did I begin to absorb that emotion?

'The Man,' as Sharon called him before she died, must have seen what Dara saw, a pretty lady. But the beauty of his love added attraction to perfection when he showed up for me day after day. He treated my children like children, as if he was respecting them as my 'kids'. He would never have considered such a question. Who does that?

This pretty lady knows her looks are fading. Without doubt, the neck has more lines now and while there is a certain beauty which comes with wisdom and age, I couldn't possibly begin to look like Jasmine. She was an utter head turner with a figure to be envied. Competition with my daughter? That was just messed up in a million ways.

I placed my back on the sun lounger and brushed the sand off as I swung my legs up to lay for a moment. Watching the white horses ferociously crash, wave after wave, I reminded myself that the world still turns, no matter how dead you are inside. I pulled my arms up above my head and looped my fingers together to hold on to the back of my skull, like Dad used to do. My nostrils flared as I felt angry at myself for even beginning to allow a tear to be a consideration. One lonely white cloud floated underneath the dark grey clouds. It was like me really. Didn't quite fit in at times, but carrying on, being carried by the wind regardless, trying to be a part of the whole plan. Life continued with its challenges, and my head carried on with its insistence in being positive. Since I read about the Law of Attraction, I felt an obligation to keep all thoughts positive to manage the good stuff. Humans are impossibly terrible at being positive all the time. Just, can't, do it.

"Hello," I heard in the distance in a local accent, being muffled by the wind. I looked down at my legs, my brown legs, my good firm legs, and swung them over the edge of the bed as I sat up and looked behind me.

"Hello."

"Oh. I am so sorry but we are having to move these. The storm, you see," he pointed to the sky.

"S'ok." I stood up and brushed off imaginary sand. I didn't actually know where I was, but I gathered my hotel wouldn't be far. Dara and I had walked and chatted for quite a while and regardless of his idiocy, that moment had just happened. Noone would take that away. Maybe he took a fancy to everyone, but I decided to choose a different thought.

Walking on the sand had made my legs ache. In the distance, I spotted a swing which was surely designed for children; perhaps. I knew it was situated just outside the resort, alerting me that I was home. Gentle specks of rain had just begun to fall from those violent clouds, and I washed my feet under the tap beside the small steps. My flip-flops landed on the floor with a slap, and I shifted my feet back and forth into the rubber soles. In the background a mix of a rhythmic base, some laughter and a cocktail being shaken mingled into each other. I took one step, then the next, and walked up to the far side of the swimming pool.

A splash was accompanied by a yell, "Louuu," in a sing song voice, full of joy. Jasmine was also in the pool. I guessed it was an early happy hour.

"Mum! Heyy-yy," she waved and smiled at me, "nice coffee?"

I continued to walk while looking at all my friends. A smile made its way to my lips, I nodded my head in approval at my coffee date with myself. Music was playing, it was time to forget about life for a while and ride the score instead.

Sitting on the edge of the swimming pool, I ordered a coconut, which took a long time for them to carve. I didn't mind at all. I was happy to just sit and wait. I watched my friends dance, some were trying new aerial moves in the swimming pool, just like in Dirty Dancing. Others were at the side of the pool, like me.

Richard headed over and sat on a sun lounger close by the edge of the pool. He was dressed and ready for the evening already. He pointed to the wet edge of the pool, where I sat, "I'm ready already. Early dinner tonight." We began an interesting conversation, as always and as he stood up to go back to the dance floor, he dropped in, "You're lovely you know." There was no meaning behind it, other than to tell me I'm lovely. Nonetheless, I still felt shy, no matter who told me.

"I try."

"No. You are. You're lovely."

43

Onward journey

Too soon, it was time to pack the big suitcases and head to the lobby to go home.

During the planning of our trip which I labelled 'the trip of a lifetime' we fathomed it might be a good idea to use the free stop off on the way home. Our airline, Etihad, drew me in to their website months earlier while we were looking at the booking pages. I wondered if I read it correctly when I saw it said we could stay over for up to two nights, for free in Abu Dhabi on the way home. In theory we already stopped off in the UEA, but I felt better getting that passport stamp, and going land side too. Did free mean free? I looked, read and looked again and yes, it seemed it was completely free to stay in the hotel in Abu Dhabi.

Packing to leave Phu Quoc carried a cloud of sadness with it. I'd felt happy there, and I could have spent more days just floating around the pool, eating the odd coconut and sleeping well at night. Some may say it was a bit of a waste of time, but to me, it showed me that life is best lived happily and in a content manner. Nothing else seemed to matter except for the feeling of tranquillity.

Friendships were formed, others were solidified, and my time with those people who were not afraid to hug each other for twenty minutes at a time filled my heart with love. They were wholesome people, and I would miss them.

Travel always comes to an end. Packing often carries myriad feelings and this was no different. Forethinking, I realised there would be a sense of 'it's over' and I agreed with my daughter to book a nice hotel in Bangkok, to stay over in Abu Dhabi and fly back on the Airbus A380. Would the plans help the feeling of heading back to the UK? I wasn't sure, but it was the best hope we had.

All of us climbed into the mini busses which were laid on for us to head to the airport and most of the conversations were muted. Energy floated around the buses, knowing this time would never be re-created. Silence sounded hollow and rucksacks became an irritation.

The short flight took us into Bangkok once again which now felt like a second home. We wandered to the luggage belt in a line of tired dancers, and while some people picked up their bags, called out and waved, others stood still with heavy shoulders and chatted about what a wonderful time we all enjoyed. There were many hugs, some lasting longer than they should, with a scrunched fist holding a jumper, and onlookers could see there was more than a friendly hug at the end of the cuddle. A few of our friends were off to travel more of southeast Asia for a while longer and a part of me was envious but I didn't seem to have the capacity to allow the thought of going with them. We had a hotel booked, which I had labelled a 'posh one' in Bangkok airport.

The two of us rolled our suitcases around the airport, in the wrong directions and back again. We tried following the map and eventually, we ended up in a hotel with grandeur and higher than high ceilings.

"Hey Peter!" We spotted a family of new friends from Australia checking in. we could keep our connection to everyone a while longer, we thought.

251

44

Swim, swim again

Pulling back the curtain to the window in the room, I faced the usual urgent ritual, while I still had the camera on. I squealed like a five-year-old seeing father Christmas.

"We have a view! Jas! The pool. Ohh look!" On the other side of the glass was a flat roof which had one panel missing from the corrugated section. Beyond the roof I spotted an aqua blue swimming pool lined with green trees and plants. In each corner were trees which I would have previously referred to as palm trees, but now I was able to look closer and know they were coconut trees. Smaller yuccas and banana leaf trees cascaded around the roots of the bigger trees. Tall blue ceramic pots stood tall at the edges of the pool, empty. White polished stones were arranged in a square around the base of the pots and further back from the edges of the pool were canvas sunbeds with rolled blue towels on the bottom of the beds. This is what our extra money paid for; a pool like this.

My delightful squeal was fuelled mostly by the traditional Thai rooves which pointed to the sky. Like obelisks, they were created to generate shade for most of us who needed it. They made the pool look as if we were in another country, so far away from London.

There was no need to unpack our cases, as we were only staying for a few hours before we rolled our cases back to the airport at dawn, before breakfast. Throwing the top of the case open, I said, "let's go swimming right now," and the heat in my body agreed this was a tip top idea.

Within minutes, we headed to the pool and wasted no time stepping into the water step by step. The surroundings were so picturesque and there was time to order a drink and take photos before starting to get our hair wet and relax completely. I began to wonder if we would do anything with these photos and videos we took. Would it all be a waste of time or would we reap the benefits of our efforts? It did feel important to me, but I was keener to capture memories too. I knew there was a chance my online efforts could pay off enough so I could continue to work, respect my illness, take care of my mother and still have a purpose in life. Often, it felt like the only way I could make life make sense; to work hard. I generated a tough exterior to give myself an illusion of being smart and brave, but occasionally there would be an air of doubt as the little girl remembered she wasn't as clever as her brother and would likely end up as one of life's failures, meandering through the floodgates of life from one 'that'll do' to another. I wanted to be a success. I wanted to ensure moments like this were not one time in life. Experiences like this should be factored in to my writing life, I hoped. All the while, keeping myself and my family on the straight and narrow.

Thoughts floated away. I was thankful. My daughter was far in the distance, on the sunbed while I held my virgin pina colada above the water, taking the occasional sip. I hadn't realised she took one of my favourite photos of the trip while I was on my own in the pool. She laid down to scroll on her phone and I floated around on tip toe in the pool, imagining this moment would last forever before I needed to face the music of a difficult life.

Clouds passed by above, just like time. Never stopping, no matter my protesting. Soon enough it was time for dinner. I hoped we could make it something special.

Eating fried rice was becoming one of those things which I knew would keep my gut safe. Was it becoming boring? Not really. I had got used to eating in batches at times. The oil they added to the cooking methods seemed to give my stomach exactly what it needed to preserve my digestive skills. Although, I did wonder over dinner if a lack of stress was also helping. There was still stress, but that was a part of who I was, but some of the moments were different to the ones at home. Would I ever sense total peace? Would I ever feel enough?

There wasn't a huge amount of time to consider those thoughts. It was necessary to get an early night before walking back to the airport for a 06.15 check in. Our flight to Abu Dhabi left at 09.15 and arrived at 12.40 their time. It wasn't long to sleep, or to be in Abu Dhabi, but I was excited for both.

255

45

Abu Dhabi; hello

Underprepared, I decided to take a deep breath and spend a few minutes working out what we were going to do. Rushing to the outside seemed wrong.

This was one country which felt like a bit of an afterthought, but also one of the places which showed promise of being the most interesting in places. It would be busy. There was lots to see and cram in. We had a few half plans, but getting to the hotel was an unknown.

The airline played at being Santa in giving away free hotel stays for those who were passing through. When I phoned the helpline, several months before from my dining room table, the guy on the phone told me they were collaborating with the tourism board to bring some people in to the country. It made sense to me. We would go there and buy our food, and we had booked a half day trip. Of course, there would be taxis and a crossing of the palm in silver Dirham and all of those added together will help the economy. No fake news, no hidden agenda, that was it. I knew we had to find a way to get to the hotel, and I had an idea our airline would provide that.

At the desk, a well-dressed woman looked as if she never stepped on a plane, let alone just step off one. I was filming everything, until we spoke to the concierge in the guest services desk. He was already frowning when we arrived, and I knew it was because of the lady in front of us. Why did money turn some people into an arse?

"Can you be quick?" she asked him with a wave of her hand as if she just touched a cobweb. He nodded over at us, and I spoke as fast as I could, asking about the transport to the hotel. Shaking his head side to side, he frowned hard and pointed to the huge glass walls in front of us where transport was pulling in, stopping for a moment and leaving again. Did this mean we needed to get on a bus?

To the left of the desk, a permanent fixture stood in a firm shade of green with the words 'experience Abu Dhabi' written on the shiny board at the top. A locally dressed gentleman was stood behind the desk and we looked over at him for a moment, wondering if he might help us. After a minute we began walking towards him, and his shoulders straightened a little. A huge TV screen displayed a film of all the local things you could do, such as a round of golf. Real live plants surrounded the desk.

"Hello, can you help us find our transfer?" I asked.

"Hello. Welcome. Where are you going?" He spoke in a slow manner and we explained the situation with our flights and the transfer. Eventually, he understood and we learned we needed to order an Uber to the Corniche district, which would cost about £26. Part of me attempted to be annoyed. I was hoping to save some money, as this had been an expensive trip in comparison to my usual work travel. But this was Abu Dhabi. We were here now, and the chance of seeing the place again would be unlikely. This needed to be embraced.

The man sweetened us with a wrapped local date. I hadn't realised the small oranges which grew on trees here were unripe dates. I was sure they were Kumquats. I felt very uneducated. We munched on our dates and Jas pulled out her phone app to organise an Uber, which was something I had never done before.

Our plan was to check in to our hotel, change and have a super fast freshen up, and go to the Etihad Towers to enjoy a mocktail and watch the sunset. Researching the views from the towers showed us this would be a fabulous sight to see and a great way to wind down before exploring with a guide the following day.

259

46

Dry, hot and prickly

Walking outside of the airport to get in our car, we noticed the polar opposite change of air. This was the hottest, driest heat we had felt in a while. My skin prickled as we left the comfort of the air conditioning and I was sure I would adjust soon. We were getting comfortable with the changes our bodies needed to deal with. Unable to see our car, I wanted to wander back inside as the heat was too much to stand, even in the shade. Jasmine encouraged me to wait there as our car was very close by. It was, and soon we were in the Uber, witnessing the new surroundings. The driver wore one glove and I was unsure why. A box of tissues was placed on the dashboard. Temperature readings from inside the car were telling us it was 54 degrees. I'd been to Egypt. I thought I knew hot. This was insane. I was thankful for air conditioning.

Drinking in the views on the way to the district where we would be staying, I noticed the width of the motorways, which seemed to have plenty of lanes for all types of drivers. I had heard there were many rules around safety in this country and everyone seemed to stick to the law. A haze hung in the air as I looked to the side of the motorway and over to a line of skyscrapers. It couldn't be mistaken or likened to anything I had seen on films, like New York; the sky was so unique as a backdrop.

We drove closer to the buildings, which were scattered among trees. The streets seemed empty as we pulled in to the driveway of our hotel, the Ramada at Wyndham Corniche. Seeing the sign was exciting, after the planning we had done leading up to this trip. I could visualise my handwriting in my diary, making notes about which dates we were travelling and where we were staying. This was our last check in, and I was ready to embrace every part of this new country.

"We have no booking," the man said at reception. I had confirmation printed out and I knew we wouldn't be stuck in a reception area in Abu Dhabi, and I knew we would find another hotel somewhere. There was a Starbucks in the corner of reception but we were excited to dump our stuff and go exploring. Two of our new friends from the trip to Bangkok and Vietnam lived in UAE and had given us a lot of tips about travelling around. Fine details were gathered about dressing for the appropriate nature of this country. We wanted to respect the rules and to also not attract any unwanted attention, so we were ready to add a few shirts to our attire and then it was time to explore.

After a short time, we were given some keys and sent to floor number ten, via the lift, which raced so urgently, there was barely time to switch on the camera. Room 1007 was waiting for us and as we walked through the patterned corridor, past the marbled floor encasing the wavy stripes on the carpet, we found our room in the corner. Corner rooms were often double aspect, and frequently some of the best.

Opening the heavy oak door, I left Jasmine to struggle with two large suitcases so I could get a real time reaction of me walking into the room. I wondered if there would ever be a time when I wasn't bothered about filming everything anymore and could just wander in with no thought except for wondering what it was like. That would really depend on book sales. YouTube was keeping things afloat and it was surely time to keep that momentum going. I was positive my audience would love to see me travel to all these areas. Knowing they were invested in my adventures could give them a good reason to tune in and I would help me to support my family while keeping active and well. I had it all figured out.

"Ohh this is noiceeee." I headed to the window, "Come on in my love, can you manage?" I looked back at Jasmine. "There we go. This is a nice sizable room," my voice changed as I moved back the net curtains. "And we've got a view. Huugh, oh yessss. Oh Jasmine!"

"Have we? Yeah?"

I didn't exaggerate. On the street below was an empty crossroads, and beyond there were a few scattered skyscrapers. Far in the distance was a hotel which I felt I had seen before on the Dubai videos and photos I had seen. Two pillars were joined at the top and I thought I had heard it referred to as Atlantis, but I couldn't be sure.

After a fast check around the room and a basic filming, we left the room and headed up to the rooftop swimming pool for a look. Chlorine filled the air as we entered the corridor which housed the door to the roof. A lifeguard sat in partial shade, just the other side of the door and the heat blasted us as we went outside. The pool was deep blue, as you might expect, in total contrast to the sandy streets below. Plenty of trees surrounded the district and we could see the seaview from the roof.

A quick change of clothes, more sleeves and we were ready to head to the Observation Deck at 300 in the Etihad towers. I had heard it was free to wander in to the Conrad hotel and go up to have a look. We had limited cash, and I didn't download the Uber app, so I was reliant on Jasmine. I felt nervous. We headed outside and remarked on the heat one more time.

47

The view

Wandering in to the Conrad hotel, it felt as if we were doing something we shouldn't be doing. I guessed it was imposter syndrome. Considering we were booked into another lovely hotel, it wasn't quite the same standard. Cars with colourful callipers passed us in plentiful supply, and the drop off area was even air conditioned which was so bizarre as it was outside. We continued to some revolving doors which kept some of the heat out. We whispered to each other. Ceilings higher than my entire house created the lounge area. The Bluthner white grand piano in front of me looked miniscule. Shiny marble floors prevented silence in this area. The lounge housed water features and I had to agree I had never seen a hotel like this before.

Pastries sat in glass fridges, all lined up with shiny fruits covering them. Truffles were perfectly lined up next door. After a brief look, I noticed there were not any labels with gluten free on them, and I decided it was time to find out how to move up 70 floors. We spoke to the lady on the reception desk near the elevators and she charged us £20 each, of which £10 was redeemable upstairs on food or drinks. Not as cheap as Thailand of course, but this was something to get used to over the next day and a bit while we were soaking up the essence of somewhere completely unique.

The lift flew up high so fast, our ears began to pop. Each floor passed by quicker than one per second, and as the doors opened, we were greeted by panes of glass from floor to ceiling, all around us in 360 degrees. In front of us was the building I thought was Atlantis, and it looked as small as my house on the ground below. The view proudly showed us the blue sea and white sand which was parading itself as if on a magazine cover. Patterns of the marina were shaped below, and the sun caught the sea in an illumination of bright light. I wondered if the Burj could possibly be much higher.

People would stand at the window edge, fully enclosed and safe, and hold on to the window frame, as if that would save them if the window gave way. We sat and opened the menu, knowing we would be sitting tight as we waited for the sun to set. Smoked Salmon sandwiches were listed as including picked yuzu fennel, cream cheese, dill butter and white ficelle bread. Fancy pants sandwich indeed. It was 65 AED, and we did some sums. We decided to just pay for what we wanted for a change; we ordered our snacks.

My nails had grown out as much as my fringe and trying to take decent photos seemed impossible. We had left home forever ago, but it now seemed as if it had only been a heartbeat since we got on the first flight. Was it really almost time to head home? I imagined the grey sky and claustrophobic buildings around us. It felt depressing. How could life feel so stressful when there are places like this to see? Once again, life felt confusing. Was it supposed to be a challenge or paradise? Undoing old scars wasn't easy when I was sitting in pure luxury, reading a menu I couldn't afford, according to my programming.

Sitting there until the sun went down was a memory I was excited to cherish. I wanted life to feel full and lived. The camera clicked more times than was necessary, but I had to capture everything. The sun caught the buildings and cast varying shades across the skyline and other towers below. We tried to fathom if we could walk to the building opposite and no matter how hard we tried, we couldn't see if there was a pathway there or not. Instead, we opened Tik Tok and did some searching to see what we should see next. Once the sun had passed the horizon, we gathered our things and descended the building in the long lift shaft once again.

A pianist sat in the lounge, dressed in a green a-line dress, just like the emoji you could find on the phone. Delighted, I moved closer to hear what she was playing and pulled out my phone to film, giving her a smile which was actually me checking she didn't mind me filming her. The ivories were playing the theme from Love Actually, which I had on a playlist of classical music in my car. I smiled as wide as my face allowed and the lady playing the piano was happy to see me appreciate her music. Above her head were several disco balls arranged in a sophisticated fashion, changing colours periodically. As the tune came to a close, she began playing Your Song, which was a tune I had promised myself I would learn to play on our keyboard, which nestled right at the back of the wardrobe. I hadn't played for years. I used to sit in my bedroom as a child and either write something, or teach myself some tunes I had heard previously. It was the two main things which kept me from feeling as though life was empty, and I wondered if it would still hold that magic at my age.

The sky turned red as we began walking towards some other building. We struggled to find the entrance and walked further than we wanted to around the streets. It was still as hot as the oven at Christmas. A bright red Ferrari scooped past with a sexy noise, followed by a matt black TVR. We saw another selection of cars including a Jeep Wrangler, a Lamborghini and a Lotus. The entrance of the hotel gave us a hint of air con which was very welcome, and the clock on the wall was a Rolex, which amused us. How much money did people have around here? It cost £517 to sleep at the Emirates Palace Mandarin Oriental, which was twice as much as the Conrad and 100% more than we paid for our free stay, thanks to our airline.

Moving in to the hotel through the lobby, we saw crystal teardrops hanging from the ceiling and knew we were in for another feast for the eyes. An air of calm was surrounding this hotel. Within a short space of time, we knew we couldn't go far into the hotel without making a reservation for food or drinks. I wanted to see it all. The hotel was so unique. I felt excited enough to find a confidence within me and ask for a menu for a bar we could see ahead. The ladies were dressed in 1950s dresses, as if they were about to take to the stage of Hollywood musical theatres. Fake trees with pink silk leaves surrounded the area and high above, glass feathers were lining the ceiling of the bar. The waitress delivered us a bowl of salted nuts and cranberries and Jasmine ordered a Sprite while I opted for a pistachio milk shake, which I felt was superbly brave of me. It was delicious. I never order such things.

The chef in me remembered from back in the 1980s just how much work it takes to create such beautiful pastries that these hotels all seemed to want to display. Taking some time to photograph the beautiful cakes, we decided we were full enough to skip a proper evening meal. Some time later, and a few more steps on the pedometer, we headed out of the hotel into a hazy evening. The lights of the Etihad towers were bringing the skyline to life, in contrast to our bodies which were ready to rest.

269

48

Exploring Abu Dhabi

Early enough, we dressed and embraced the day ahead, with the first stop being the Sheikh Zayed Grand Mosque. On the plane, on the way out, a documentary had expertly captured the making of the Mosque and I was even more excited to see the wonder of this piece of architectural history.

Social media was full of amazing pictures of this building with its egg shell appearance and as our one gloved taxi driver pulled up to the building, we could see it in its entirety. Such a sight to see, like nothing you would expect to see on your regular daily commute. This place seemed interesting and aside of the heat, we were excited to get out and explore.

"Be back here at the 1h40minutes, so that's erm," he checked his watch and gave us a time to be back at the car. He looked at my outfit, which had been expertly planned. A frown appeared as he seemed unsure. I had long baggy trousers and a t shirt, high up to the neck and a shirt over the top of the t shirt. What was wrong? I even had practiced covering my head with my pashmina, which was a gift I was given by my new husband in Venice on our honeymoon many years before.

One thing I wanted to pride myself on was respecting the cultures around us. Heck, I had even resided with a Muslim family and got close to marriage at that time. I knew how important it was to be mindful and I was ready.

"They might let you in, if not, you will need to buy one of these type of things," he gestured with his hands to show me a hijab, "which will only be about $20/$30" I wasn't too keen to spend money on something I would never wear again, but there was no way I was going to muss the tour of the mosque, so I embraced whatever was to come and stepped forward to the line of people who were to be inspected.

Long upright signs, like barracudas were displaying what was and wasn't allowed in regards to dress. It was strict and I had no issue with that. It seemed we were appropriately dressed and Jas and I helped each other to cover our heads. We were not used to this. It helped you to stay hot, and we would have to deal with that for a short spell of time. Over the course of the past couple of weeks, we had got used to getting sweaty. At home, that would have been unacceptable but in the countries we had been, it was just the way it was. Ok, it was our time. Behind the lady who was inspecting us was another barracuda, explaining that you were not allowed to take photos inside, unless there was a particular sign saying you could. Our research had shown us that already. We knew that. Images of humans hugging or making hand gestures such as peace signs were not allowed anywhere in the mosque.

The lady in front looked at me. As I expected, she called out something which I didn't understand, over to a gentleman dressed like a corporal. Exchanges of words and nods of the head went on and she wafted her hand to the side of her, telling me to go through. I was relieved but I had kept calm. I had done nothing wrong. I would have worn whatever they wanted me to wear. Both Jas and I began walking in the same direction as the crowd in front of us. More signs alerted us to the rules, and we decided to make a point of remembering them all. I was glad of the air con, which we knew would come to an end soon. Thank goodness this was early in the morning. Apparently the best time to go to avoid big queues for the photo pit stops.

Heat was falling out of the sky already, despite the early time. Several people were in front of us to visit this huge mosque. Around us were fountains, water features, the biggest carpet in the world. We stopped to read more about this splendour which was written on the wall:

The Sheikh Zayed Grand Mosque in Abu Dhabi is a marvel of modern Islamic architecture, seamlessly blending tradition with contemporary design. Completed in 2007, this grand structure is one of the world's largest mosques, with space to accommodate over 40,000 worshippers. Its pristine white marble domes and minarets create a striking silhouette against the desert skyline, symbolizing peace and spirituality. The mosque's 82 domes, 1,000 columns, and stunning reflective pools add to its serene beauty. Inside, visitors are greeted by the world's largest hand-knotted carpet, intricately crafted in Iran, and awe-inspiring chandeliers inlaid with Swarovski crystals that radiate a warm glow. Known for its commitment to cultural inclusion, the Grand Mosque is open to visitors of all faiths, inviting them to witness the exquisite artistry and reverence embodied in every detail, from the floral mosaic courtyards to the calligraphy inscriptions celebrating Allah's qualities. This architectural gem serves not only as a place of worship but as a bridge between diverse cultures, showcasing the splendour of Islamic art and the spirit of unity it promotes.

Stepping into the entranceway of the Sheikh Zayed Grand Mosque, I felt the desert heat gently ease under the mosque's cool, sweeping archways. The stark white marble glistened under the sun, and as I lifted my gaze to the rows of domes against a blazing blue sky, I was struck by a sense of reverence that transcended the heat pressing down all around. My trousers brushed the floor, picking up some of the dust, as I walked, blending me into the serene flow of other visitors who had come to marvel, to reflect, or perhaps to find some quiet peace in this magnificent place. The moment I stepped fully inside, the air was still and calm, like a protective sanctuary from the world outside. The silence seemed magnified by the expansiveness, drawing me deeper into the quiet beauty that lay beyond, beckoning me to explore.

As I moved further into the vast square of marble that opened beyond the entrance, I felt as if I had entered another world entirely. The courtyard, known as the Sahan, stretched out in every direction—a gleaming expanse of white marble inlaid with colourful floral designs that felt both delicate and immense underfoot. My daughter, walking beside me, marvelled at the sight with wide eyes, her reflection shimmering faintly on the polished surface. The midday sun was intense, yet the brightness of the marble seemed to absorb and diffuse the light, casting a soft, almost ethereal glow across the open prayer area.

We found a spot near one of the arches, and I pulled out my phone, positioning us so that the mosque's majestic domes framed our faces. I snapped a photo of us together, ensuring we were not touching each other, our smiles slight; blending with the serene beauty that surrounded us. Capturing this moment felt both special and almost surreal. Here we were, mother and daughter, standing in one of the most stunning places on earth, the elegance and scale of it all humbling us both. After each photo, I'd turn and look out at the sweeping courtyard again, savouring the sight, wanting to capture more than just images—a feeling, a memory that would stay with us long after we'd left. I was afraid I would forget this, or not appreciate it enough.

A sharp voice came from the side of us, just as we were adjusting for another photo. I noticed a middle-aged Chinese couple nearby, visibly delighted as they posed together in front of the mosque's grand arches. The woman leaned into her partner, and he slipped his arm gently around her shoulders, a small but intimate gesture that seemed to capture their awe and happiness in the moment. Almost immediately, a guard in a pristine white kandura approached, his expression polite yet firm. In a quiet but direct tone, he explained that physical displays of affection were not permitted here. The couple quickly separated, their smiles fading slightly as they nodded in understanding. The guard's gentle but unwavering reminder served as a powerful reflection of the cultural respect this place commanded. Watching the couple quietly adjust, I felt a renewed awareness of the balance this place struck—welcoming to visitors, yet rooted in customs that spoke to its deep spiritual reverence. I tucked my phone away for a moment, realizing that here, more than anywhere, every gesture mattered.

One foot after the other took us through the majesty of the place, and I was reluctant to find the end of this palace. Realising we were close to the end, I dabbed my forehead with my pashmina. Umbrellas were at the entrance and exit of every archway. They were for sun protection. I had always grimaced at people using those in the past. Until now, when I grabbed the wooden handle and opened the umbrella to give me some shade. The heat felt like tiny bee stings on my skin which was unpleasant yet endearing. Things were different here and I liked to embrace the change. Jasmine suited the scarf around her head in a majestic, royal appearance. She was stunning in this early light.

We hopped on a fast golf cart for the return walk along a long corridor. Scarves still firmly attached to us, the wind created by the speed was a welcome cooling breeze. After we stopped off, we noticed a vending machine like nothing I had ever seen before. Oranges were inside and you could put some money in and watch the oranges be squeezed into a cup, and served to you In the tray below. It was refrigerated, and my body craved the sweet, cold juice. It was the best orange juice we had ever tasted.

Shops lined the outside part of the mosque which showed the difference between trade being accepted just outside of the mosque. Hijabs were on display, covered in jewels and sequins, just like some which a lady was wearing inside the mosque for a photo shoot. They were over £700 to buy, and we walked on past. I also walked past the cup and saucer which had expertly painted skylines and the words Abu Dhabi on them. I knew this would be a welcome addition on my desk as I was now carrying the label of Travel Writer, as I filmed for TikTok each morning. But I decided not to spend the money and walked past with instant regret which remained for longer than needed.

Our driver was waiting in the underground car park, with the other people who were in the car with us before.

"Did you not be able to find us?" He asked in his Indian accent.

"No. We knew where you were. Are we on time?" I asked, knowing we were not late. Jasmine softened my response as if to halt me.

"We just had a little look in the shops."

The driver turned back to face the front of the vehicle, put on one glove and started to drive us to the next destination.

Parking near a line of shops, I remembered Turkey. Even though they labelled a visit to the shops as an excursion, it was a way for the tour guides to make more money. The 'tut shops' as I called them were always full of rubbish to buy. But this shop was different.

"Ah, welcome, welcome! Please, come in and enjoy the cool air," the shop owner greeted us warmly, his smile broad as he gestured to the colourful displays around him. "Here, we have the finest dates in all of Abu Dhabi! Medjool, Ajwa, Khalas—each one sweeter than the last. You must try a sample; our dates are fresh, full of flavour, like little bites of desert sunshine!" He picked up a beautifully wrapped box, holding it out proudly. "Perfect for gifts, or maybe just a treat for yourself. Please, look around, and if you need anything, I am here!"

Before I had realised, I must have tried six different dates and I had become a fan and a connoisseur. Buying dates would be foolish, as we would be flying home within 24hours. So, we enjoyed what was on offer and encouraged the other tourists to buy some things, which they were happy to do. I was keen to move forwards and was glad to get back into the cool car and drive through the hazy streets towards the Atlantis hotel once again.

Just past the hotel was a man-made village called Heritage Village.

As we arrived, the bustling energy of the modern city seemed to fade away, replaced by a sense of quiet history. The air was warm, carrying with it faint traces of incense and spices from nearby stalls. Traditional mud-brick buildings and palm-thatched huts were nestled around us, recreating the simplicity of a desert village from generations past. I watched artisans at work, crafting pottery and weaving textiles, their hands moving with practiced precision as if time had hardly touched these ancient skills. Nearby, a camel waited idly, adding to the authenticity of the setting. The contrast between the towering skyline we'd left behind and this reimagined Bedouin life was striking, and I felt as if I had stepped back into an Abu Dhabi that was long gone but lovingly preserved. Heritage Village wasn't just a museum, it was a living tribute to the roots of Emirati culture, inviting us to connect with the spirit of the desert.

It was a little hard to fathom the total point of this place, other than to see how they used to live. I guessed it was kind of like a museum. Without doubt, it opened my eyes to see how life would have been before the invention of air conditioning. I couldn't imagine how humans could survive. My little irritations seemed insignificant in comparison.

Beyond the walled confines of the village was an opening which glazed over past the image of what I would imagine paradise to look like. The sea was a deep marine blue, and the sun gleamed off the white sand so much I had to adjust my sunglasses. Moment after moment I called out 'wow' into the camera on my phone as I was filming and taking photos. Without any hesitation, we took several photos and knew it would all look outstanding on Instagram later.

Soon enough, it was time to head back to the meeting point to find the driver, who was stood next to the car under the shade of a short tree, talking to someone else who looked like a driver. Our minibus had a big silver reflector in the window to help keep it cool. The driver saw us coming and moved his feet from under the shade as if he was burning.

"Oh, one minute please." He opened the sliding door and ran to the other side of the car to start the engine and fire up the air conditioning. My forehead was omitting sweat faster than I could cry, and the air con would have been very welcome. The driver began to remove the shade in the front, and said, "ohhh, hot," as he threw it to one side and reached on to the dash to grab his glove. As he fixed the glove onto his left hand, I realised its purpose. The steering wheel would be too hot to handle, so instead the drivers wore a glove. It all made sense to the English woman who was used to wearing gloves to keep warm.

The driver glanced at me in the rearview mirror, a knowing smile on his face as he navigated the quiet streets. "June is the off-season here," he explained, his voice warm but matter of fact. "Not many tourists come because, well, it's too hot! The temperatures can go over 40 degrees Celsius, sometimes close to 50. People prefer to visit in the cooler months when the weather is kinder, and they can explore without melting." He chuckled softly, as if remembering how drastic the summer heat felt even to him.

He paused, then continued with a thoughtful look, "You know, Abu Dhabi is home to so many people from all over the world, mostly here for work. In fact, more than 80% of the population is made up of expatriates: Indians, Pakistanis, Filipinos, Egyptians, and so many others. They come here for jobs in construction, hospitality, business, you name it. There's an opportunity here, especially in a city that's growing as fast as Abu Dhabi. It's like a blend of cultures, all working together to build this place." He nodded as if to himself, then added, "But in summer, it's mostly just us locals and residents toughing it out, waiting for the cool season to bring the crowds back."

I thoughtfully looked out of the window and pondered how interesting it was that the place was largely full of expats. While I could see why, I also found it fascinating to see how we all expected the streets to be paved with gold here, when in fact, I was craving a coffee in a coffee shop with my laptop. Was I becoming a creature of habit? That thought frightened me and I turned my attention back to the driver.

"Where's the others?" I referred to the tourists.

"Oh, they went back so they were collected by another driver," he said.

"Oh ok. So where next?"

"A quick stop for some photos first."

We were back at the same hotel we could see from our room. A line of palm trees cascaded from the street up to the hotel and parallel to that was a water feature stepping down towards us. Dolphins made of some shiny metal 'jumped' up the steps as we stood in turn to take photos of ourselves. The driver offered to take one of both of us, and graciously I said yes, knowing I would prefer my own selfie as always.

49

Coffee

The tour was over, and we were dropped back to our hotel. We asked the driver a hundred questions on the way, to ensure we made the best of our limited time there. He said all shops were closed during the day as it was too hot. We may find a few cafes open but nothing else. It was all starting to make sense. It was literally too hot to function.

We asked him to point out any cafes on the way back, but we didn't manage to see any close to the hotel, so when he dropped us off, we took ourselves step by step forwards and ended up not far from the hotel in a café called Hamton café. My mood made me smile; my shoulders dropped as I relaxed. This felt like a familiarity which I was happy to welcome into my reality for a short while. We were hungry and wanted to explore the menu to see what I could eat.

On the table was another box of tissues and compartments surrounded it which housed the sugar and sweeteners for the coffee. A waitress brought us two bottles of water before we had pulled in our chairs beneath us and I did some mental maths, wondering about the cost. This was a ritual here and it was needed, so the couple of extra pounds on the bill would be essential. I would have to stop worrying for a short while. A 'call' button was in the middle of the table which was something we needed to push when we were ready to give an order. The waitress didn't hover, instead she returned to the serving area which had the words Hamton Café illuminated over the top, nestled within a living wall. The toilet area also had plants surrounding it, the air conditioning was tip top, the chairs were comfortable and the people inside the place were working on their laptops. I felt at home and was happy to sit for a while and eat something good. We ordered chicken wraps. I knew I would have to pull the chicken from the wheat containing bread, but I didn't realise the chicken was also breaded. I ate the chips and left the rest for Jasmine. Drinking my coffee and water, I was fulfilled enough to remain happy, calm and reflective as we planned the rest of our afternoon.

I had heard about Soul Beach, a pristine stretch of white sand along the Saadiyat Island shoreline in Abu Dhabi, and I was debating whether it was worth a visit. Everything I read described it as a slice of paradise, with crystal-clear, turquoise waters gently lapping against the sand, and lounge chairs neatly lined up under large, shaded umbrellas. It sounded peaceful, a true escape from the busy city and a perfect spot for soaking up the sun. But then there was the question of the heat; it was June, after all, and the sun was unrelenting. I wondered if I could manage the midday rays, even with the sea breeze. People said the beach had a calm, relaxed vibe, almost like a private resort, and it offered a chance to unwind, maybe even dip into the refreshing Gulf waters. Part of me was already picturing myself there, toes in the sand, taking it all in, while the other part weighed the scorching temperatures and whether it was worth enduring for a few blissful hours. I knew it would make excellent Instagram photos, and I was excited to make as much content as possible in the time we had, in the hope I could take my travel adventures into a full time role. I wanted people to see what you can do if you put your mind to it. After learning the law of attraction, I felt life was a blessing and a curse.

We decided to go.

285

50

Soul Beach

Throwing a few things in to some bags, we picked up the phone and scrolled to the Uber app and ordered another cab. As the car arrived, we took photos, it was so luxurious. I wasn't sure of the make, but it made my dream car at home look like an old banger.

The ticket price to get into Soul Beach was £20 each. The staff fixed wristbands on to us but didn't give us any towels. That was it. There were people without wristbands on the beach. We felt ripped off but I knew we were doing the right thing, we only had an hour to sit there and enjoy the views which were like something from a luxury TV advert. I had never seen such a stunning beach. The contrast of blue sky, blue water and cream coloured sand was the most perfect image my camera had ever shot. White umbrellas enjoyed the blue-sky backdrop and I knew we would be able to gather some fabulous images here. I was glad I had worn my new orange bikini with the golden pineapple metal ties on the ends. Braving the sea, which was warm, I covered enough of my body as I squatted in the sand and sat on my legs. Above my waist was exposed to the air, and the camera, just as my bikini top was. As if I was posing for page three, I embraced the moment, knowing I would never be this young again. Instagram response was favourable a few days later, as I blushed, wondering if this was inappropriate.

My daughter wore a stunning bikini with way less fabric than mine. Every photo I took of her was either showing her back, or her looking off into the distance. She wouldn't look at the camera and I gathered she was just being artistic.

Fifteen minutes sitting on the sunbeds in the shade followed, as we listened to the group of lads next to us having a great time laughing together but it was soon time to get another Uber back for a quick change as Jas had booked to go driving on the Formula 1 racing track, and I would be filming it.

51

Racing

Another taxi, another journey for half an hour in air con. More maths as we figured if it was worth us taking our things and staying at the track after the race. We were close to the airport which we would fly home from on the airbus A380 at 2am. The race was at sunset, which was around 6pm. But we embraced the cab fare and left our things at the hotel. It seemed easier.

As the sun dipped below the horizon, the Yas Marina Circuit transformed into a breathtaking scene of lights and shadows. The iconic F1 track, with its smooth, winding turns and gleaming barriers, glowed under a sky streaked with fiery oranges and soft purples. The grandstands, sat empty. I could imagine cheers echoing in the cooling desert air. Overhead, the track's neon lights began to illuminate, casting a surreal glow on the asphalt and creating an atmosphere of electrifying excitement. The unique architecture of the Yas Hotel, with its shimmering LED canopy, came alive against the fading daylight, adding a futuristic touch to this world-class racing arena. At sunset, the Yas Marina Circuit wasn't just a racetrack it was a dream coming true for one lady. The noises roared from the track, as one car circled the tarmac. A traditional racing car carried one excited forty something woman around and around as Jasmine fitted her racing suit on, with two plaits cascading her sohulders. She looked stunning in anything, and I was excited to see her drive. Her buzz was contagious.

It took some effort to stop myself from being over-protective. I wasn't quite sure what she would be driving or how fast, but my concerns were rested when the instructor pointed me to the viewing area which overlooked a go kart track. Plenty of twists and turns showed off the challenging nature of the track, but I was glad it wasn't the main F1 course.

Watching Jasmine climb into the little car, I saw a small girl, who had legs too short to reach the pedals. The instructor used hand signals to tell the drivers to start their engines and Jas waved her hand in the air as casually as she could, but she was clearly a little anxious. He came back to the car and adjusted her pedals so she could reach, and she was off. She looked forwards. I climbed the stairs to the viewing area. As I reached the top, a sharp pain carved its way through my tummy. I held my c-section scar area and let out an audible 'ohh'. Taking a deep breath, I exhaled, and the pain subsided. Taking one more step, I wiped my top lip with my index finger and looked at the track to find my daughter. It was impossible to see who she was, so I enjoyed watching and filming, while willing her to finish safely. The roar of the engines was never my favourite noise, but I felt a sense of pride in my daughter. She wanted to do something, she researched, she booked it, and here we were. I was so glad she knew how to enjoy her life.

Another pain hit my womb area, and I felt as if I was on day one of my period. I tried to ignore the pain and used breathing as a coping mechanism, but it got stronger before it subsided again. Focusing back on the track as far as possible, I paid attention to the bright lights and the fading sun. the sky was looking more beautiful by the minute.

Twenty minutes later, the chequered flag was raised and wafted in a figure of eight as the drivers filtered in one by one. It was almost time for the sun to set on our trip and fly home. I was thankful this moment was in my reality. The trip was more than I had imagined, and we had already imagined it was going to be amazing. I wish we felt as if we had been gone away for ages, but it hadn't seemed that way. It had just felt like a couple of weeks in southeast Asia and Abu dhabi. We were so blessed, and I felt immensely fortunate to finally do something so exotic. Considering the money mindset I was raised with, and carried with me, I was making it happen. I knew I wanted more of it.

One little lady climbed out of the Go Kart, and I picked up my things and walked down the stairs. To my right was a podium.

"Don't you get to stand on 1st 2nd and 3rd?" I asked.

"Well, I didn't come 1st 2nd or 3rd did I?" Jasmine said as she let out a chuckle. The pain came again, and it felt like a poker into my belly. My hand reached down to cradle the pain as I frowned.

"Oh Mum, are you ok?" Jasmine asked me.

"You don't have your period, do you?" I had read somewhere

about girls all moving towards their cycles at the same time. I wasn't sure why I asked the question really, after losing my cycles suddenly, following a shock, several years earlier. Perhaps I was feeling her cramps.

"No." Her eyes held a shadow of concern. But I brushed off the pain and suggested we go to the dressing room to get her back into her clothes. She was roasting from the inside out in her racing gear.

Again, the cramp hit me like a stealth wave: a fierce, sudden grip low in my abdomen that stole my breath and made me clutch my middle. suddenly, my vision clouded, and the track seemed to fade into a distant hum. A cold sweat broke out across my forehead as the pain spread, twisting itself deeper, sharper, until I had to sit down, gripping the edge of the leather couch.

The room was filling with people excitedly chattering about the race, but all I could focus on was the growing knot in my stomach. I took a few deep breaths, hoping it would pass, but each breath made the pain sharper. I felt a gentle hand on my shoulder, and a voice, low and calm, asked if I was alright. I must have looked pale because the next thing I knew, someone was on the phone, calling for assistance.

"No, No, it's ok. I'll be ok, thank you." I breathed through the pain. "I have a plane to catch soon," I said.

Soon after Jasmine was changed, Paramedics arrived. I noticed a blur of uniforms and medical gear, I was carefully lifted onto a stretcher as they secured me tight. I was using the same breathing techniques I had used in labour as the pain drove me in and out of consciousness. I glanced back at the track one last time. I saw Jasmine moving toward me.

"Mum?" she said.

"I know. It's ok tho." I was delirious with the pain and unable to make much sense. I could remember we were due to being flying back home soon.

"What happened?"

"This lady," I pointed and used kind words to explain she was worried.

"Come on," Jasmine said as she grabbed my hand and walked alongside the stretcher. I knew I was going to be ok. I was not particularly in a panic. The ceiling faded to black before I left the building. The heat from the air brought my consciousness back once again as we headed to the ambulance.

The ride was short, though every bump and turn made the pain flare up again. I felt woozy by the time we arrived at the hospital, where the bright, sterile lights greeted me. I was taken straight to the emergency room, surrounded by clean white walls and the subtle, almost medicinal smell of antiseptic. Nurses flitted around, checking my vitals and asking questions about the pain as I tried to answer between shallow breaths. After what felt like an eternity, a doctor approached, holding a clipboard and peering at me through gentle but concerned eyes.

"It sounds like you're experiencing severe abdominal cramps," she said, her voice steady. "Let's run some tests to rule out anything serious. We'll do a pelvic ultrasound and take some blood work to check for any signs of infection or inflammation."

I nodded, feeling a strange sense of relief just hearing someone put a plan into words. Within moments, I was being wheeled into another room for the ultrasound. The technician was calm, walking me through each step of the procedure. I focused on the screen, watching the grainy black-and-white images flicker. I tried to decipher them, but they were just blurry shapes and shadows.

Back in the emergency room, I waited anxiously, every minute feeling like an hour. Finally, the doctor returned with a compassionate smile, holding a set of results. "Your tests show that it's most likely a condition called endometriosis, which can cause intense cramps as you're experiencing. It's when tissue like the lining of the womb grows outside of it. I'd recommend starting you on some pain management right now and discussing longer-term treatments with a gynaecologist, as there are various options, from hormonal therapies to, in some cases, surgery if the pain persists." I listened, trying to absorb the information through the haze of discomfort and fatigue. She handed me some pamphlets detailing lifestyle changes that could help, like diet adjustments to reduce inflammation, and recommended that I follow up with a specialist soon.

"Wait a minute. I knew this already. I had surgery when I was just 21 for endo. I know all this."

"Ok, interesting. Seems it would be a flare then."

"But it's been years since I have had a period. I had early

menopause, due to a shock."

I felt a strange mixture of relief and anxiety. They gave me a prescription for some pain relief and suggested I stay hydrated and rest as much as possible over the next few days.

"Let me just mention that to Dr Khaled," she said as she left the room.

After a short while, a tall man in a white coat approached, holding a tablet and peering down at me with a calm but concerned expression.

"Hello, I'm Dr. Khaled," he said, his voice warm and soothing, with a gentle Middle Eastern accent. "I understand you're experiencing severe abdominal pain."

Dr. Khaled glanced at his tablet and pulled up the ultrasound images and shifted his gaze to meet mine, his voice still calm but laced with empathy.

"The ultrasound showed something we didn't initially expect," he began gently, his words measured. "There's an empty sac in your womb. It could be a sign of a condition called a blighted ovum, sometimes known as a phantom pregnancy."

The words hung in the air, weighty and confusing, and I searched his face for an explanation. He continued, carefully choosing his words to keep them both clear and comforting.

"A phantom pregnancy," he explained, "occurs when the body shows all the symptoms of being pregnant, but there isn't a developing foetus. It can be caused by an imbalance in hormones or, in some cases, a misinterpretation by the body, almost as if it 'believes' it's pregnant." I knew it was impossible to be pregnant. Other than my hormones, it had been almost two years since I said goodbye to the man I was in love with. No one came near, physically or emotionally.

The feeling was hard to describe. I'd come to the hospital expecting to find a reason for my pain, not to learn of a condition I hadn't even considered. The idea of my body preparing itself for something that didn't exist was surreal and unsettling.

Dr. Khaled leaned in, his calm, steady gaze anchored on me. "It's surprisingly common, actually," he said gently, "and it can be emotionally challenging, especially when you experience real symptoms; cramps, even nausea or swelling without a true pregnancy. Your body's response can feel very real, even though there's no viable embryo developing in the sac."

He paused, giving me time to take in the information, as my mind tried to wrap around the idea. I felt a strange sense of emptiness; a space where a certainty I hadn't known I was holding had suddenly been replaced by confusion and a hint of sadness.

Dr. Khaled's voice softened further. "Sometimes, with a phantom pregnancy or a blighted ovum, the body can take time to recognize what's happened. Your symptoms might continue for a little while until your body naturally resolves it. Or we can offer medical assistance to help move things along if the symptoms become overwhelming."

I nodded slowly, trying to hold onto the reassurance he was offering, even as the implications washed over me.

"Thank you for explaining all this," I said, my voice barely a whisper. Dr. Khaled nodded, his warm, compassionate smile returning.

"Take it one day at a time," he said. "You're not alone in this. Many women go through similar experiences, and it's important to process it at your own pace. Be gentle with yourself, and if you have any questions, don't hesitate to reach out."

The weight of the news settled over me, accompanied by the surreal sense that my body had been preparing for something that would never be. I couldn't quite find words for it yet, but Dr. Khaled's kindness and patience made it feel possible to move forward, one careful step at a time.

The term "phantom pregnancy" seemed both haunting and strangely fitting. I'd heard of it before, but I'd never thought it could happen to me. *How could my body believe something so deeply without it being true?* As the weight of it settled, I found myself replaying the moments from the past few months, moments when I'd brushed off my symptoms as stress or changes in routine, even though part of me had felt different. Could my emotions have played a part in this? Perhaps I was feeling the effect of impending empty nest already. He leaned back in his chair, watching me with that familiar calm expression.

"I get the feeling," he began gently, "that you have more questions than answers right now. If you'd like, I can explain a bit more about how a phantom pregnancy can sometimes be influenced by psychological factors."

I nodded, grateful that he understood.

He spoke slowly, as though carefully building each idea. "Our bodies and minds have a powerful, sometimes unpredictable, relationship. In many cases, a phantom pregnancy, also known as pseudocyesis, can develop not only from physiological factors but also from psychological ones. Sometimes, when there's a deep emotional desire or fear surrounding pregnancy, the mind can, in a way, 'convince' the body of its reality." He looked at me, gauging my reaction before continuing. "It's more common than you might think, especially in people experiencing big life changes or emotional stress. The brain's response to that desire or anxiety can, quite literally, create symptoms."

The idea that my own mind could trigger such an intense response in my body was disorienting. I had never imagined my inner world could have such power. "So it's like my mind believed I was pregnant, and my body followed along?"

Dr. Khaled nodded. "In a way, yes. For many people, this happens almost subconsciously. Some research suggests that the mind, in its attempt to cope with emotional needs or stress, can signal the body to produce pregnancy-like symptoms. Hormones might shift slightly, causing real physical changes: weight gain, nausea, and even lactation in some cases. And for others, the belief can be so strong that they feel the symptoms just as intensely as they would with an actual pregnancy."

I thought back to the months leading up to this. I'd been wrestling with uncertainty about the future, mixed feelings about relationships, and an increasing sense of isolation as the children were growing up. It was always my plan to have a big family, but that was not meant to be. Had my mind, in some way, taken all those swirling emotions and directed them inward?

Dr. Khaled continued, his voice gentle and reassuring. "This isn't a matter of willpower or a lack of awareness, it's the body's natural response to intense emotional states. In cases like this, I usually suggest talking with a counsellor or therapist who can help you explore these feelings. Not only to process the experience but also to understand what underlying needs or fears might be there. Addressing these can be incredibly helpful for both physical and emotional healing."

Hearing him say it that way made the idea feel less foreign, less like something was "wrong" with me. Dr. Khaled's warmth and lack of judgment allowed me to feel safe exploring these feelings, knowing they were part of a natural, but weird, response.

As I left, I felt an unexpected lightness, like a small weight had lifted. The ache in my womb and the strain on my mind were still there, but knowing the connection between them helped. I knew I had healing to do, physically, but also mentally. Understanding this journey would allow me to find a new balance between my mind, my body, and everything I had yet to discover about myself.

Stepping back into the heat, I clutched my paperwork and felt a sense of gratitude for the paramedics, the doctors, and even the stranger at the track who'd noticed my distress. It was important to become even more honest with myself and self-aware and admit that I was grieved to be watching my children break away from me. Was this normal?

I had given them my all over the years, to the detriment of my own relationships and now I was going to be alone, so close in the future.

My time as a Mum was the most precious gift I could have wished for. I was sure I had raised two wonderful people, and I had loved every minute. My life was designed in whatever way it was. And I was forever thankful for being a Mum. Without them, would I even be here?

Somehow, I would have to let them go and let them soar. Hiding my pain was impossible. The only way forward was distraction. Could I begin living the purpose I felt I was put on the Earth for? Would I be blessed if I was making moves towards my writing dream? Could it be fruitful enough to continue forwards in life, paying the bills, and changing lives?

Meeting Johanna had shown me I was not the awful person I had been raised to believe I was. Simon's chat had assured me even the most talented people start somewhere, this episode in hospital had shown me I needed to move on. Flying solo in life gave me the opportunity to sit and write, change lives, focus on creating the books I was designed to create.

52

Airbus

We sat in silence at the airport. It was busy, except for the space around the little robot dancing to a Michael Jackson tune on the floor. My pain relief medication was making me comfy, but drowsy. Jasmine was looking after me now. Tables had turned. She helped me check in my passport and loaded my case onto the belt. It was time to head home. The trip was over.

Sleep took over the next few hours as I decided the Airbus was just the same as all the other planes, sort of. Life felt hazy and unfamiliar. I didn't know what was next.

53

Home

Being home was comfortable.

I text Sandy. I followed up with a voice note, explaining that I had decided I was to embrace the writer life. I knew she would be overjoyed as she had suspected in my spirit that I was being guided to write from every angle, and until I listened, things would continue to happen. I pressed send on my phone, and followed with an afterword of plans,

"I will carry on with my job at uni, as it's only part time and only September til April really, and the in between times, I will write. It feels good and right. That's what I'm going to do. Oh, and I'm excited for the publishing show next week."

On a technical level, there were things I needed to learn. Audio books were taking over as a preferred method of reading, and I needed to get on board with creating those books. I had tried, but I failed. There was a little technical hiccup which I needed to address, and I knew there would be experts at the show who I could speak to. Brilliant!

Attending the conference in the previous two years had given me the motivation I wanted to push me forward. Money was holding me back. And they kept saying, by not putting audio out there, you are 'leaving money on the table' and I wanted to produce more income, so it would acceptably be considered my job. There were no desires to get rich, or famous, but I did need to be able to take care of my family, and myself in the coming times. Embracing the need to up my game felt like natural progression, and I was excited to leave my anxiety at the little corner of my bedroom and go to London to meet some other people who would be my future.

Out of my comfort zone, I browsed the posts which were flooding in to the group chats as I walked to the meeting point on the Tuesday evening. I needed to know where I could find people. Was there more than one bar in that pub? I knew they were 'at the back' but where was that? I had to grow up. There were people with real anxiety, way more than I was experiencing. They would never look at me and consider for one second I was not confident and highly successful. All such a lie.

Deep breathing exercises were helpful and automatic as I walked through the sunny London afternoon. Thoughts flowed through my mind to remind me that this was both a dream, and a necessity. Sandy was right, life would keep throwing me curveballs until I listened. I was designed to be a writer and no matter how hard I tried to fill my time with 'real' jobs, there was only one thing I was supposed to be doing. People referred to it as my hobby, my passion, but seldom did they call it a job.

Clocking in a 9 and clocking out a 5 was not a path I felt comfortable with. So many things about it felt wrong and aside of which, working with other people, with all these scars on board was no good. I ended up upset with people, or afraid of people. When I wasn't with people, I wanted people. When I was with people, I was scared shitless.

There were the other people who asked over and over, "you're always on holiday," or "what holidays have you got booked?" I offended easily, Dad said. But it was my work. I reviewed and filmed hotels as my profession, and now I had decided to write about those life experiences for many reasons, mostly to show that bad things happen to us all, and hopefully instil a little faith in people. I wanted them to realise we all go through things and yet we will be ok. I'm ok, kind of. And if we can all raise our vibration just a little, perhaps we heal the planet. I heard recently, while navigating a new hypnosis and meditation course, when boxing matches are shown on TV, the rate of murders increases. Instantly, I thought, 'energy' and my mind came back to me being a writer, helping people feel better, and healing the world. I'm not ever going to be Ghandi, or Dr Wayne Dyer, but if we all did a little bit, surely, we could help.

One foot followed the other I the late afternoon sun and I hoped not to arrive too sweaty.

The corner of the street appeared, and I saw the pub. The exterior loomed ahead, its dark, weathered bricks and Victorian-style signage giving it an air of mystery that both intrigued and unsettled me. I pushed open the heavy wooden door, feeling a sudden waft of warmth and the faint, cozy smell of aged leather and wood polish. Inside, the light was dim but inviting, casting a gentle golden glow over the bar's rich mahogany countertops and the scattered tables tucked into small, intimate corners. My eyes adjusted slowly to the interior, and as I took in the scene, I realized how aptly it had been named: *The Mad Hatter.*

The place was lively and chaotic, filled with the low hum of conversations and the clink of glasses. I could see faint touches of Wonderland-inspired decor—whimsical clocks on the walls, odd (but charming) mismatched furniture, and intricate vintage lamps casting soft, shadowy patterns on the ceiling. I hesitated, half-expecting to see a grinning Cheshire Cat around the corner, and feeling the familiar nervousness rose in my chest as I scanned the room for a place to sit. There was nowhere, so I found a friendly face and began walking towards her.

At the bar, a group of locals laughed with the bartender, their laughter blending with the strains of a mellow rock song that played in the background. A large, winding staircase curved up from the back of the room, leading to an upper level I couldn't quite see but imagined was just as eclectic as the ground floor. Despite my initial nerves, I felt a strange sense of belonging here, like I'd stepped into a secret place that welcomed anyone willing to embrace a touch of whimsy. A perfect place for writers to meet.

Near the fireplace, small, framed portraits of people were framed in elaborate hats and old-fashioned garb. A small menu sat on the table, with handwritten chalk illustrations that only added to the pub's quirky charm. I glanced around once more, taking a deep breath as the initial nerves started to ease, replaced by a quiet excitement to explore this curious little slice of London.

"Hey, I'm Lou," I announced without a quiver.

"Hello and welcome. Your first time?" She asked, remembering our Facebook messages. It was my first time. Many others went to this meet up, the night before, in the years previously. But I wasn't brave enough. This time, I felt more focused, as if I was becoming a proper writer, which was ironic as to be a writer, you just had to write. But my purposeful nature had arisen by a series of events and now it was time. I needed to try and work the room.

Chatting to another non-fiction author, I realised just how diverse 'non-fiction' can become. My books can carry tales which are inspired by the truth but shouldn't be factually quoted. This author needed concrete facts woven through his books.

Aware I was only talking to one person, and keeping him from talking to anyone else either, we moved away from each other and ended our conversation. Just like in dance, there should be light and shade. Did I really need to rush to the next person? Or could I stand for a moment and just be in the room? Opting for the latter, I soon made a new friend. And I bloody loved her.

"Come on, sit over here." She said and held out a flat hand in front of her, "have you met this lot?" She proceeded to introduce me to everyone before squealing in delight as one other person pulled up. She held her hand up to the edge of her lips and spoke from the side of her mouth as if this was a secret, "he was only up on the bloody stage last year! Fuck!" She chuckled. I really liked her. She was awesome. I wanted to spend more time with her. I liked her gentle swearing and confidence. She was more confident than me. That was unusual.

After everyone seemed to get back to their usual friends, I felt it would be time to head home. Even though I could have put a hotel stay through my business, we still were not quite making enough money for my accountant to justify hotel stays. So, while they all sat between the wonky tea pots on the walls, drinking, I headed back to the train. Excitement for the publishing show was ever present and I walked up to the table to sign in the next morning.

"Oh, you're Lou," I heard above me.

"Yes?" Fame already? That was one thing I didn't want.

"I live near you. We should get together and maybe do some writing sessions or something."

"That would be fab wouldn't it. Set something up."

"You set it up. I'll join in with my wife," he said. And I did that right away. We were building communities.

After using the toilet for the lucky wee that I didn't really need, I bumped into my awesome friend from the night before. She remembered my name, without looking at my lanyard, which was so impressive. Once again, she talked a lot, which I really liked! She told me all about her fiction book and the success she was having with it. Despite only writing one day a week, she had managed to get a famous bookshop window for ten days and a signing. That was the stuff dreams were made of, that was what I wanted.

"How did you sort that out?"

"I just went in and gave the manager a copy of my book, asked him to consider helping promote it, as I am a local author."

"I might do that, you know." I said. I began to ponder that idea and realised I needed more books out before I could start promoting myself. I was taking a new direction, and my formatting and editing would be more professional next time. I could absolutely put a Waterstones window on my wish list. Perhaps a signing. Who knows, maybe in future 'an audience with,' could feature in my reality. I pondered this idea over the next couple of days as we absorbed the beauty of the conference and what we were learning. Things began to feel possible.

54

Magic

The speaker at the publishing conference had words on the back of her T-shirt which drew my attention. My eyes seemed to glow at the words. Illuminated, I could feel this pathway was guiding me once again and I knew I would only be able to ignore it for so long before something even more drastic happened.

She turned her back to me and the typewriter typeface said something about storytelling. I needed one of those T-shirts. It would be able to accompany the tote bags I was given on the way in which was announcing to the world that I am stepping into the version of me who is a committed writer.

My university job needed a lanyard. There were people fighting over you wearing their representation of the university lanyard. We had the plain uni ones, the LGBT, the disability network, the alumni, the list was as long as it could be. I chose to wear my publishing conference lanyard from the previous year. Remaining grounded, this reminder of who I was, even if I was in denial, was an excellent way for me to feel better about this life. My bracelet had a dangling quill. Wearing this while I was teaching in my science job at the

University helped me to ensure I would not lose my vision.

To wear one of those T-shirts with 'storytelling' written on it, would be another label to affirm my wants.

The coffee break arrived, and I skipped into the welcome hall where all the partners were. Like a seven-year-old, I presented myself to the tall guy who was on the stand.

"Your colleague in there had a t shirt on. I need one of those in my life."

"Oh." He didn't look me in the eye, but he looked behind him and giggled at the same time. "We don't have any," he said as he looked behind the barracuda.

"Never mind, it was worth asking anyway."
He began to tell me more about the company and signed me up to their email list and some apparent prize.

"I'll probably win, I'm lucky like that, I always win things." I told him all of that, without hesitation or doubt. After coffee, I dashed back into the hall, knowing it was time for them to announce the winners of the social media sharing competition. The doors banged into the wall as I entered too fast, and I started to run down the steps as if there was nothing wrong with me. Two seconds after I set my backpack on the chair, I heard,

"And a lovely video was made by this person, do we have Louise Usher?"

"Oh, that's me!" I called out as if I was completely expecting to win. I won a t shirt, and while I was hoping for the Kindle Paperwhite, I had just been off manifesting a free t-shirt, so that's what I got.

The next coffee break took me off to chat to the team at Spotify, who were generous with their time. Along with being an author comes a stack of technical needs. Audio is becoming a huge area for growth within part of the author world, and I had tried and failed to upload some audio books. Asking them my technical questions, they were able to instantly pinpoint what I needed to do, and the epiphany was overwhelmingly exciting. I was ready to head forward into the world of knowing the next step in my writer world. I was excited.

"Would you like one of these tote bags?" They asked as they held up a canvas bag with Spotify written on it, and a visual of a stack of books. Genres were listed on the spines of the book images, and I was delighted to see 'non-fiction' written there too.

"Oh yes please, I would love that."

After a slow evening dinner with an old friend, we walked the sunny Southbank and ate ice creams which were £9 each. A wholesome day had given me reasons to smile and feel positive as I headed into the days to come.

Victoria train station was busy, and chaotic, which was poles apart from my excited mood.

I found my train and walked up the aisles to find a seat. During the fast walk through the train station, I had been filing ideas in my head into their compartments. There was money, ambition, needs, and family. All being sorted and sifted. I had decided I would continue with my part-time hours teaching at the university, to help with a bit of income, and the rest of the time I would be focusing on my writing projects. I voice noted Sandy again, who I knew would be delighted. She always told me the stars aligned for me in the writing world, and I should not be ignoring that voice.

5.02 the train departed from London.

5.03 I picked up my phone to check my emails. There was an internal email from the university, advertising many new positions. They were advertising my position. *My* job, the job I invented. The position I had been doing for three years. As I read on, I could see twenty full-time positions were being offered.

Anger ran through me. I had just decided to stay in my job part-time and now I *HAD* to go full-time. It would be a lot to juggle both. But I had no choice. Mortgages need to be paid, and I would have to go full-time.

In an instant, I emailed the HR department, asking if I needed to complete the application form and go down the usual route, considering this was a role I created from nothing. I rested my hand on my chin and looked out of the window at the city and the flashing sunbeams between buildings. This was annoying, but nothing would derail me from my dream. I enjoyed the best couple of days, and I knew exactly what I needed to do to move my writing career forward. I *HAD* to keep on those right tracks.

My jaw clenched as the streets of London flew past the train window. How was this possible? I was so excited to become the writer I had dreamed of being and I knew the academic world wanted their pound of flesh. Could I even write anything if I was working full time as a lecturer? The job would be more of a challenge than I could handle. Health, Mum, being a Mum; it all felt overwhelming. My head buzzed and I felt my mind being erased of all the good things I had sucked up the past two days. I wanted things to stay the same. My part time hours were ideal to support this writing world.

The phone pinged with an email from HR who said yes, I should apply for the role, otherwise I would lose my hours. I put the phone back on the table with a heavy hand and accepted the fate.

After the incredible feedback I had received from the students, academics and head of operations, I knew this job was going to be mine, and I wondered if they might ask me to head up the other 20 people. I wasn't sure I could do that too.

The following morning, after sleeping on the news, I felt calmer, and even a little excited. The fixed salary would bring security and a certain income. This made sense. I would be able to transfer from the interest only mortgage I had been locked in to for 18 years and get a repayment mortgage. Sensible. And while there would only be 5 weeks holiday each year, maybe I would be able to figure a way to continue my travel writing, but I wasn't convinced that would be enough time to sustain a business. I could try. I could figure things somehow. And the extra earnings could perhaps pay for a cleaner and more carers for mum so I could focus on just work, and only work. I felt excited. This was a role I would love, and I could get my teeth stuck into. The writing dream could stay in the box I'd put it in for many years. It wasn't sensible.

Working hard on the application, I passed all three parts of the process until I reached the final stage interview which took weeks but was very positive. At the end of the interview, the lady asked if I had any holiday booked, if I needed to work any notice, (considering I was already working there) and if I wanted full time or part time. I didn't hesitate to opt for full time, as my mind had done the sums over the weeks from first application until final interview, and I was excited to finally earn a decent wage. The children were older now. Perhaps it was time I grew up too.

Days passed and I refreshed my emails more times than was healthy. Jasmine was waiting to book an event which we usually went to together. But it fell on 'welcome week' at uni, which would be a significant week in my calendar as all the new students arrived. I said she would have to book without me, as I wasn't so sure I would be able to get the Friday and Monday off.

Five days later I was fiddling in the kitchen. The bench had a new faux fur on it which I was shaking to fluff it back up. An email sound came from my phone, and I checked right away, it was news about the job, I could tell from the subject line.

"Ohh," I said out loud and cradled my phone into my chest.

"Is that it? Is that about the job?" Jasmine asked. I nodded and sat down to open the email.

'You have been added to the reserve list and we will be in touch again when everything is sorted.'

What? What on earth did that mean? My heart was beating hard and my insides felt electrocuted, a familiar feeling I had from the past when I discovered I was cheated upon. Same really, I guess.

Immediately and angrily, I called the head of HR who was apparently a bit of a fan of mine. She explained, "600 people applied for 20 roles, so you are lucky to have got this far, you've done well, but there are people with more experience."

"People with more experience? I have been doing this job for the past three years. Does previous track record does not account for anything?" Apparently, it didn't. And that was that. All I could hope for was to keep the hours I was previously working.

After three difficult months of worry, waiting for an answer, I found out the job was completely gone. They wouldn't be taking me back. Apparently, something to do with the new government. I didn't understand.

55

Dickens

My diary was once again a saviour as I sat in the shade of Dickens's house and wrote:

'All of these years, a whisper has told me to write. Now it's time. The opportunity has come; I'm thankful and I feel blessed. I know, with all of my 'self' that this is my purpose.
A little chip in the rockface, granted, but a shiny diamond, nonetheless. Finally, this is my time to write more, publish and perhaps inspire people. Writing saved me, many times and it was a hand-holding best friend when I needed it. Over and again, the pages and the pen showed me the way. When no one was there, I had words.

Along the way, in 2011, I wondered if I could reach out to another online platform, in the hope of sharing my message. I turned to YouTube, which was 'only for the brave' back then. I knew somehow this would be a platform for voices to be heard. My content was focused on the law of attraction, making life better and doing things the best way possible. Then I took my camera and my small audience to Egypt. More people flocked to my channel, and I accidentally became a travel vlogger. I adore creating videos. My channel is now sailing; it has potential.

Here sits the writer, with stories squirming to make their way to publication and distribution, I want that. I also want to travel; I seem to want it all. I am organised. I am single. I could have it all. But; focus.

Surely to focus on one thing would be of benefit. People have been confused for years as they come to me for help with health, manifesting, how to write a story, running their writing retreats, speaking gigs, booking trips and the most FAQ: which room did you stay in when you went to Tunisia?

Do I really have to choose one or the other? They are both stories crafted from travel. One is on a page; one is a video. Perhaps a few more late nights in the office, with autumn candles lit, could see me do both I like the idea of making a success of both. If I *HAD* to choose one, it would be books. Do I have to choose one?

Things are shifting. I have been asked by an art gallery to run writing for wellbeing retreats. I mean, I can do that.

Here on the jetty, it's special. I feel very emotional, I could cry.

As I look up at Bleak House, I imagine Charles Dickens sitting there in his window, writing in the still of his day. I could cry, I've realised with fabulous, undeniable gusto that I just want to write by myself and it's the strangest feeling to realise it. I'm emotional at the open sense of knowing one's authentic self. The realisation of coming home to who I am has just hit home and tears want to flow, can't flow. I sit with peppermint tea and sweet potatoes, overlooking the bay of Broadstairs, and I am brimming over with emotion. How lucky am I to get to realise what my total passion is?

Word to myself: I need to write, publish and sell books. It must be done and from a place of getting it done. I want to embrace all of that now. I want to write by myself. I'm not too fussed that I lost the job, it's only money. And money is ok.'

I took a sip of my mint tea and felt something brush my leg. A little dog was at my feet, and I asked the owner, who was sat behind me, if I could pat the dog. She didn't respond, so me and the dog decided it would be fine. I loved feeling the soft fur. There was time for such things now.

Embracing the creative in me, I picked up my pen once again, as the base of my eyelids contained the tears which were forming. I took a deep breath as I looked across Broadstairs Beach and let my eyes rest on the colourful buildings up on the prom. Clasping my hands together, I leaned my head on my wrists for a moment. This was it now, it was time.

I wrote in my diary once again, a short, creative piece that felt as if it wanted to surface.

'Sandy sinks:

Times at the beach; time passing like the tides, the best of times. I wash my hands in the stainless-steel sink, spotting sprinklings of sand surrounding the taps. I remember those happier times of my girlhood when we would float all day. At the beach today, working on the next book, the muse wades in, like the surf, as I lift my gaze to the house. Charles lived there. He wrote in the window, overlooking the sea, writing 'David Copperfield' in the quiet of his solus. I could cry. The still of his day evokes my emotion. Beneath the house, I sit to write.'

"There's no Wi-Fi here if you want to work," the waitress said. "No, that's ok thank you," I said as I put my pen on top of its case. I signed off from my writing session with a note to myself: 'Right must dash to sort out mum, where did I put the toolbox, the fence needs sorting before I go…'

Louise Usher

About the Author

Louise Usher is an international number one bestselling British author. She's also a blogger, YouTuber and entrepreneur. She is known for her work in the self-help and personal development genre. Usher has written several books, which aim to inspire and empower individuals to achieve their goals and live a fulfilling life.

In addition to her writing, Usher runs a successful website where she shares her personal experiences, insights, and tips on various topics such as mindset, motivation, and entrepreneurship. She also offers coaching and mentoring services to help others overcome challenges and reach their full potential.

Usher is passionate about helping people transform their lives and believes in the power of mindset and positive thinking, with a great deal of realism thrown in. She often emphasizes the importance of self-belief, goal-setting, and taking action to create the life one desires.

Through her work, Usher has gained a loyal following and has been able to impact the lives of many individuals seeking personal growth and success. She continues to inspire and motivate others through her travel and life writing, coaching, and online presence.

Her work centers around Life Writing of modern day challenges. Motivational, inspiring stories often come from her own experiences, and at times through talking to others who have a story to tell. She encourages journaling, automatic writing and scripting for manifestations. A unique approach to storytelling but popular with all who love biography and fly on the wall.

www.louiseusher.co.uk

Acknowledgements

Wherever we go, stories unfold.

The chattering mind and I begin as a pair, with an idea for a narrative. The circle widens as people, places and perspectives weave their tapestry into a story.

The following people contributed to the creation of this book, allowing the story to flow to you.

Huge thanks and love to my twins who always play a part in this narrative called life, but especially to my son for stepping up and taking care of the mundane stuff so I could find a tale to tell. Thank you to my wonderful 2nd born, who navigated with me, carried the cases and was a constant advisory for the creative marketing and formatting of this book.

I'm grateful for the select few who encouraged me to step into my writing world full time, with a leap of faith, and still sent messages when I was shut away writing by candlelight, surrounded by neglected housework. Shona, Hannah, Shah, Sally, and Jack; thank you for the reminder I'm not alone.

As for my writing clan, I've been motivated by all of you at SPS every year. I have huge gratitude for my writing buddy, Emma who loves coffee almost as much as I do.

Travel creators came into my life with a bump this year and helped me sit up extra tall as we realised how magical elephants are. Laura, Ryan and Amy thank you for your kindness and belief in my dream.

Also by the author:

https://amzn.to/3OioYZS

https://amzn.to/40R6MOA

https://amzn.to/3UZUC2m

https://amzn.to/4fvqsvP

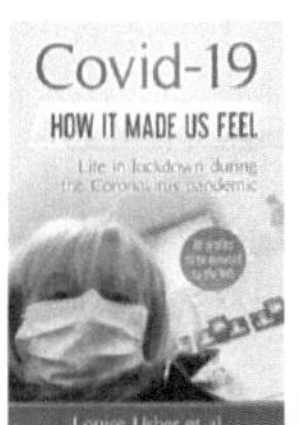

https://amzn.to/3YRS1IY